KT-495-569

'This is no paddling-pool approach to prayer. R.T. presents the simple basics while inviting us to explore the depths of communion with Almighty God, our Father. Simple, comprehensive and thoroughly motivating, this book fills in the gaps left by so many publications on this vital topic.'
Colin Dye, Senior Minister, Kensington Temple, London

'What an amazing, insightful, delightful, revelational, instructional, motivational, powerful book on a subject that all of us need to understand and practise more. Dr Kendall has done it again: Taken a truth that I need more revelation on, and opened the windows of heaven! This book on prayer is a must read for every person who desires to move more of heaven to earth.'
Robert Morris, Senior Pastor, Gateway Church, Texas.

'R. T. Kendall has done it again. He has combined theological clarity with spiritual depth to give us practical insight on how to pray and grow in our relationship with Jesus. The great need of the hour is to grow in prayer and R.T. has served the Body of Christ well in giving us much needed inspiration and instruction.'
Mike Bickle, International House of Prayer of Kansas City

'Since the spring of 1956, R.T. and I have enjoyed a "David and Jonathan" relationship forged during a spiritual awakening at Trevecca Nazarene College, following lectures by Methodist evangelist John R. Church. R.T. was

my student assistant and pastor of a small Nazarene church in Palmer, Tennessee (near Chattanooga). One Monday morning, returning to Nashville, he was agonising in prayer, when he received a life-changing baptism with the Holy Spirit. Sharing his experience soon after that created in me a thirst that eventuated in a fresh infilling of the Spirit that permanently deepened my life in Christ. R.T.'s prayer life is unquestionably the well of both his anointed preaching and writing. This book reveals the heart of R. T. Kendall.'
William M. Greathouse, General Superintendent Emeritus, Church of the Nazarene

'This is a fantastic book, perhaps the best I've read on the subject. It's challenging, forthright, practical and has deeply affected my own prayer life, so thank you, R.T.'
Lyndon Bowring, Executive Chairman, CARE

Did You Think To Pray?

Also by R. T. Kendall

The Anointing

The Christian and the Pharisee (with David Rosen)

The Gift of Giving

Great Christian Prayers (compiled and edited
by Louise Kendall)

In Pursuit of His Glory

Out of the Comfort Zone

Pure Joy

Second Chance

Tales of Total Forgiveness (with Julia Fisher)

Thanking God

The Sensitivity of the Spirit

The Thorn in the Flesh

Total Forgiveness

Totally Forgiving Ourselves

Worshipping God

Your Words Have Power

Did You Think To Pray?

R. T. KENDALL

HODDER &
STOUGHTON

Unless indicated otherwise, Scripture quotations are taken from the
HOLY BIBLE, NEW INTERNATIONAL VERSION.
Copyright © 1973, 1978, 1984 by International Bible Society.
Used by permission. All rights reserved.

First published in Great Britain in 2008 by Hodder & Stoughton
An Hachette Livre UK company

2

Copyright © R. T. Kendall 2008

The right of R. T. Kendall to be identified as the Author of the Work has
been asserted by him in accordance with the Copyright, Designs and
Patents Act 1988.

All rights reserved. No part of this publication may be reproduced, stored in a
retrieval system or transmitted, in any form or by any means, without the
prior written permission of the publisher, nor be otherwise circulated in any
form of binding or cover other than that in which it is published and without
a similar condition being imposed on the subsequent purchaser.

A CIP catalogue record for this title is available from the British Library

ISBN 978 0 340 96409 5

Typeset in SabonMT by Avon DataSet Ltd, Bidford on Avon, Warwickshire

Printed and bound in Great Britain by Clays Ltd, St Ives plc

Hodder & Stoughton policy is to use papers that are natural, renewable and
recyclable products and made from wood grown in sustainable forests.
The logging and manufacturing processes are expected to conform to the
environmental regulations of the country of origin.

Hodder & Stoughton Ltd
338 Euston Road
London NW1 3BH

www.hodderfaith.com

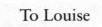

To Louise

Contents

Foreword by Ken Costa

The measure of the importance of this book is that R.T. has taken his time – twenty years – before writing on that basic Christian subject: prayer. This gestation project has produced a gem. It is mined with precision from the biblical texts, polished through personal experience, and cut to reflect the intensity of God's desire for us to pray. This is a rare jewel.

Did You Think To Pray? is a down-to-earth, practical and challenging work. R.T. does not pull his punches as he motivates the reader to spend more time with God daily in prayer. With pastoral sensitivity and understanding, he encourages all Christians to make prayer a priority in their lives, to spend time with God, and to know his 'ways'. Through a lifetime of personal experience of prayer he deals with the many questions that prayer raises, and in honest and frank anecdotes of his own struggles, successes and failures, he guides the reader in how to live a life of prayer.

Prayer is squeezed out of our busy lives. Here is a real incentive to get back to God, on our knees, to take him at his word and to see our lives changed. This book is a 'must read' for the busy and spiritually hungry person.

R.T.'s ministry and his writing have had a profound effect on my own life, and I regard his book on the life of Joseph, *They Meant it for Evil but God Meant it for Good*, as being one of the most formative books I have ever read. His latest book, his fiftieth, is no exception.

Ken Costa
Chairman, Lazard International;
Churchwarden, Holy Trinity Church, London;
Chairman, Alpha International

Preface

A few weeks before we left our home in Florida, I suddenly felt an impulse to write a book on the subject of prayer. 'This can't be the Lord,' I thought. 'What publisher would want to print another book on prayer? There must be thousands of books on prayer,' I said to myself. But the urge to produce this book became so strong that I went to my computer and started writing, literally putting to one side two other books I had started to write. My writing flowed, and in a day or so I had written thousands of words.

One week later my editor in London, David Moloney, phoned me with something on his heart. 'R.T., have you thought of writing a book on prayer? I have been thinking about this for a good while.' I was 'gobsmacked', as we say in England. So was David when I told him I had a good chunk of it already written!

The truth is that I started to write a book on prayer

twenty years ago. I wrote a chapter or two, then gave up. I just wasn't ready for it. But I always wanted to write such a book, and here it is.

This will be the last book whereby David Moloney will be my editor – in that he feels called to move on from Hodder & Stoughton to do other things. They will miss him, and I will miss him. He has been a wonderful editor and friend.

We have recently moved from Florida to Tennessee, having always said that if we didn't live in Florida we would want to be in Nashville. We now live on Hickory Lake – full of bass rather than bonefish – in Hendersonville, a suburb of Nashville.

This is my fiftieth book and, coincidentally, on 28 June of this year – 2008 – Louise and I will celebrate our Golden Wedding Anniversary and fifty years of married life. The time is long overdue for me to dedicate a book to her. I did in fact dedicate my first book (*Jonah*) to Louise and our two children, but this is the first one dedicated to her alone. It is doubly appropriate that this book be dedicated to Louise, for I know of no other person who has a greater prayer life or love for prayer than she does. Thank you, Louise, for being my wife for these fifty years. Thank you, Lord, for giving her to me.

R. T. Kendall
Hendersonville, Tennessee
February 2008

Introduction

The men of Israel . . . did not enquire
of the LORD. (Josh. 9:14)

I have had a head start when it comes to prayer, because the earliest memory I have of my father is seeing him on his knees for about half an hour every day before he went to work. Part of that time was spent reading his Bible. He was not a minister but a layman, a rate clerk for the freight train division of the Chesapeake and Ohio Railway Company in Ashland, Kentucky. It was a usual sight for me to see – my dad on his knees – as I got ready to go to school; I came to assume that praying in that way was the normal, natural thing to do.

While shaving, my father listened to a daily radio broadcast from the Cadle Tabernacle of Indianapolis, Indiana, that came on at 6.15 a.m. Every broadcast was introduced by someone singing the following: ''Ere you left your room this morning, did you think to pray?'

The earliest memory I have of my mother was much the same thing. When I was four or five, before I started school at the age of six, I can recall feeling fed up that I had to wait every morning for her to finish her time of prayer. She graciously ignored my protests of 'How much longer?' and finished her time with the Lord, lifting her hands in the air as she knelt in worship to God.

Not only that – my mother prayed with me each morning before I went to school, although this time we stood up to pray just before I went out of the door. But if one of my friends dropped by a minute or two early, my mother – to my chagrin – would invite them in to be prayed for as well. Even though her prayer lasted less than a minute, I was always embarrassed when it involved my friends.

As a youth, when visiting evangelists came to my old church in Ashland, and I heard how some of them had very strong private prayer lives, it moved me so deeply that I wanted to be like them. There were two particular men – Glen Griffith and Spencer Johnson – who, though regarded by many as strange, seemed to me to have the most power in their preaching. I then found out that they prayed several hours every day. For reasons I still cannot explain, hearing about their private prayer lives gripped me no end.

When I was about fifteen, I developed my own prayer life. I didn't discuss it with my parents or anyone else. I just found myself wanting to pray more and more – as often as I could. I did not think there was anything unusual about it – praying for fifteen minutes every day before I went to school, then another fifteen minutes at night before I went to bed. I always knelt in front of my rocking chair when I prayed. Kneeling when praying was the main way we were taught as I grew up.

It was not until years later – at the age of nineteen – when I became the pastor of the Church of the Nazarene in Palmer, Tennessee, that I began to realise that I was not a typical teenager and that my father was different from most church members. I sensed that teenagers under my ministry were not the slightest bit interested in spending much time in prayer and that most people in the church did not spend time in prayer in the way that my father did. In fact, it was not until I was the minister of Westminster Chapel in London, when I asked every member to spend thirty minutes a day in prayer (including time reading the Bible), that I realised that this was regarded as 'unfair' by many of them.

'Thirty minutes a day?' one of the older deacons remarked. 'I don't know what to say after five minutes.' His comment made me feel that perhaps I was being unfair and that I should not place these demands on my members. I then began to feel guilty. Even my wife Louise thought I should stop asking people to pray so much. (I will return to this subject later in this book.)

My father had a prayer list. He prayed through that list,

adding to it all the time, every day for years and years. He eventually memorised it. After retiring at sixty-five, his prayer life increased considerably. Instead of thirty minutes, his prayer time extended to an hour, sometimes two. But this of course was in his retirement years. His wife Abbie (my stepmother) told me that when they drove somewhere, for much of the journey he would sometimes pray out loud – praying his prayer list from memory. One day she began to count the items as he would pray for people by name and their situations. She counted over five hundred. She had no idea he prayed for certain people, some of whom neither he nor she had seen for a very long time. I can remember when my father first visited us in London, and he came with me to Pontefract in North Yorkshire where I was preaching. He took an interest in the pastor there, Bill Dyer, and his family. He wrote all their names down, and I can recall him asking me about them two or three years later.

At the age of eighty-five, my father got Alzheimer's disease. But for a few years before he died, at the age of ninety-three, his long-term memory was still good. I asked him about everything I could think of. One day I said, 'Dad, please tell me something. Why did you pray so much? As far back as I can remember, you spent more time in prayer than most ministers. Why?' He replied: 'When Gene Phillips came to be our pastor in Ashland, he asked every member to pray thirty minutes a day. I did what he asked us to do and kept it up.' Soon after my father died on

1 April 2002, just two months into my own retirement, Abbie ordered his tombstone, which you can now see at his grave in Fitzgerald, Georgia. On it are the words: 'A Man of Prayer'.

This book is not intended to be a eulogy to my father, or to sound pious, or make anyone feel guilty. But now you know my background, you will perhaps be patient with me in my emphasis on the *amount of time* we spend in prayer. I know of no other book on prayer that stresses this.

Shortly before leaving Westminster Chapel for 'retirement' in February 2002, I was asked to address one hundred London ministers at Holy Trinity Brompton. They gave me ten minutes to speak on the subject of 'prayer', so I took the ten minutes to urge every one of those ministers present to spend no less than *one hour a day* in prayer (not counting sermon preparation, etc.). It seemed to be greatly appreciated by those there, and many of them thanked me profusely.

A few years ago a poll was taken among clergy in Britain and America asking them to reveal (anonymously) various things; among the questions was 'How much actual time do you spend alone in your quiet time before the Lord each day (not counting sermon preparation or praying with people)?' If you do not already know the answer, what do you suppose is the average amount of time a typical church leader, vicar, minister, priest or pastor spends alone with God every day?

Before I reveal the results of the poll, listen to these

words from Martin Luther's Journal: 'I have a very busy day today, must spend not my usual two hours – but *three* – in prayer.' John Wesley was up every morning at four o'clock to spend two hours on his knees before starting his day.

I don't mean to sound unkind, but where are the Martin Luthers today? Where are the John Wesleys?

According to the aforementioned poll, the average church leader – on both sides of the Atlantic – spends between *four and five minutes* a day in quiet time with the Lord. And we wonder why the Church is powerless!

Children spell 'love' T-I-M-E. What if God spells 'love' T-I-M-E?

When you and I stand before God at the Judgement Seat of Christ, we may have many regrets concerning how we spent our time. But I think I can safely promise that you will not regret any amount of time you spent in prayer – alone with God.

In the time of Joshua, the people of Israel were not prepared for the way they had been deceived by the Gibeonites. The Gibeonites became a thorn in Israel's side for many generations. But it need not have happened. The cause was put simply: 'The men of Israel sampled their provisions but did not enquire of the LORD' (Josh. 9:14). A huge mistake could have been avoided – if only they had prayed first.

O what peace we often forfeit,
O what needless pain we bear,
All because we do not carry
Everything to God in prayer.
Joseph Scriven (1819–86)

I write books in order to change lives, and I pray that this book will change your life. I hope to make the case that the amount of time spent in prayer alone with God matters. I pray it will grip you from the crown of your head to the soles of your feet, and that you will never be the same again.

PART ONE

What Prayer Does

1

What Prayer Does for God

The LORD would speak to Moses face to face,
as a man speaks with his friend. (Exod. 33:11)

Evangelist J. John told me about a trip he made to India
a few years ago. Shortly after he arrived, he heard
about a saintly lady called Sister Theresa (not Mother
Teresa) and was told she had a powerful gift of words of
knowledge. J. John got to meet her and asked her, 'If you
have a word for me, I would be so grateful.' He said that
she turned around and left, and he feared he had offended
her. But she came back to him an hour or so later with a
list of thirteen items (some of which bowled him over
because they were so accurate), ending with these words
that he will never forget: 'God likes your company and asks
that you give him two hours of your time every day. That's
all. Goodbye.' Wow.

J. John took her seriously and, I can tell you – because he has told me more than once – he was never to be the same again. I personally think it explains, at least in part, why J. John is one of the greatest evangelists today – not just in the United Kingdom, but throughout the world.

What does prayer do for God? For one thing, he likes your company.

I cannot imagine a greater motivation to pray – that God enjoys having me in his presence. He enjoys my company and delights in listening to me! He doesn't get bored with my repeated requests, and he doesn't moralise if I get it wrong in what I ask for. He doesn't laugh at me if I put silly, even impertinent, requests. He never makes me feel stupid. There is no rejection, only total acceptance.

It doesn't get better than that. Said David, 'How precious to me are your thoughts, O God! How vast is the sum of them! Were I to count them, they would outnumber the grains of sand. When I awake, I am still with you' (Ps. 139:17–18).

When God speaks to us face to face, as he did with Moses, it is impossible to say who enjoys it most – God or us. I am moved to know that God spoke to Moses face to face, 'as a man speaks with his friend' (Exod. 33:11). God loved Moses' company; he loved Abraham's company, also calling him his friend (Isa. 41:8; James 2:23). What a compliment to the disciples that Jesus said to them, 'I have called you friends' (John 15:15). Friendship is developed by spending time with a person.

4

The thought that God likes my company thrills me more than I can explain to you. And if he likes my company, he likes yours too – he is no respecter of persons (Acts 10:34; 1 Pet. 1:17). The same blood that purchased Peter's and Paul's salvation bought yours and mine. Moreover, it is that blood which gives all of us equal access into God's presence (Heb. 10:19). I therefore can put out of my mind the thought that some people are more acceptable to God than others. One's profile in the Church has nothing to do with our being accepted by him – or loved, or enjoyed. We are all on level ground. Nobody is at the head of the queue because he or she has a higher profile in the Church, has been a Christian a long time, has been on a forty-day fast – or is famous. Being a head of state gives you no leverage.

As St Augustine put it, God loves every person as if there were no one else to love. I hate the thought of being a bore; I hate wasting people's time. I can sometimes tell by the look on their faces if they are not happy to see me. I fear rejection. And if I'm not careful, I can carry this fear of rejection right into the presence of God, assuming I am boring him too. Why should God care about *me*? Why should he listen to what I have to say? And why would he like my company?

It is such a dazzling thought, that the same God who has countless billions of angels worshipping him sixty seconds a minute day and night, to whom the nations are but a drop in the bucket and who knows all about every leaf on every tree in the world, also *welcomes my company* – because I am very important to him.

Indeed, I can think of no more amazing thought than this, that God loves me as much as he loves Jesus. That's right! You and I are co-heirs with Jesus (Rom. 8:17). Jesus even prayed that we would grasp that the Father loves us just as much as he loves Jesus (John 17:26).

If there is anything that will make us blush in heaven it will be the realisation of how much we were loved on this earth – but didn't appreciate it. And if we knew how much God welcomes us when we turn to him, we would almost certainly pray more than we do. God likes our company.

What does prayer do for God? It blesses him.

We must never underestimate the privilege that is ours in offering the quick prayer, the utterance made urgently in a time of need – in crisis, or when we are on the move. We've all done this, and God is the first to come forward to say that he is an 'ever-present help in trouble' (Ps. 46:1). So he is OK with us doing that. He never holds a grudge, as if to say, 'Wait. You cannot talk to me now. Where have you been for so long? You are only calling on me when you are in trouble.' The truth is that God may even *use* the trouble to get our attention.

In this book I have therefore chosen to focus quite a bit on *time* with God, the longer moments. And if we realised how much he likes this, I am sure it would motivate us to spend more time in his presence – doing nothing but talking to him.

In Part One of this book, called 'What Prayer Does', I have chosen to show first of all what prayer does for God. But perhaps you thought I should begin with what it does for *us*?

I might have done this, but our generation is so 'me-centred' anyway that I wanted to write a book on prayer that is 'God-centred'. Instead of asking the question 'What's in it for me?', I want you to ask, 'What's in it for God?' And the irony is that we get more from him than ever this way! This is because God only wants what is best for us.

But he is a jealous God. If you want to get to know the true God – the God of the Bible – you have to come to terms with this fact about him. He is 'upfront' about it – he admits to being jealous. Many of us don't want to admit to jealousy of any kind, lest it show our insecurity – or dignify a person we don't want to admit to being jealous of. But God says it in the Bible: 'Do not worship any other god, for the LORD, whose name is Jealous, is a jealous God' (Exod. 34:14).

I find this encouraging. Instead of being resentful that God is jealous, we should be thankful that he is like that. It shows he cares! It shows he wants all he can have of us, that the Spirit of God he put in us jealously yearns for us with a love that will not let us go (James 4:5).

> *O love, that wilt not let me go,*
> *I rest my weary soul in Thee;*
> *I give Thee back the life I owe,*

That in Thine ocean depths its flow
May richer, fuller be.
George Matheson (1842–1906)

Have you ever wondered why God cares so much for us? David asked the same question, 'What is man that you are mindful of him?' (Ps. 8:4). Why does God have a *special* concern for *human beings* as opposed to plants, animals, fish – and the rest of creation? There are at least three reasons for God's jealous care over us: (1) we – not *any other creature* – are made in God's own image (Gen. 1:26); (2) God's eternal Son (before the eternal Word was made flesh) chose to take on *not* the nature of angels but the seed of Abraham (Heb. 2:16 – Authorised Version); and (3) Jesus died indiscriminately *not* for animals or angels but for every human being (Heb. 2:9).

Whether you are a believer or not, you are bought with a price (1 Cor. 6:20; 2 Cor. 5:15). Yes, even those who do not submit to his lordship are none the less *bought* with the blood of Jesus. Peter referred to those who actually denied the Lord who 'bought' them (2 Pet. 2:1), referring to people who never were truly converted. This means that God has sovereign rights over each of us – saved or lost.

But when we gratefully acknowledge that the blood of Christ turns God's wrath away from us (*propitiation* – Rom. 3:25; 1 John 2:2 – English Standard Version) and washes away all our sins (*expiation* – Rom. 5:9; Eph. 1:7), we thus consent to his right to us. This means that God has, if I may put it this way, a *treble reason* for wanting our attention. First, we are justly his by creation. Second, we are rightfully his by the death of his Son for every person. Third, but when we *affirm* the blood of his Son, he has the ultimate reason to be involved with us.

Not everybody acknowledges Jesus' death on the cross. He died for all, but not all believe in him. So when we *recognise* that we are his by virtue of his Son's blood, God has a further reason to love our company. We should therefore welcome his every overture towards us in wanting to spend time with us. What a privilege! And what a thrill it is that the King of the universe actually wants to spend time with you and me.

What prayer does for God, then, is that it affirms him when we acknowledge the most important thing he ever did: sending his Son, the Lord Jesus Christ, to die for us. The first prayer we ever utter – when we understand the way of salvation – comes down to these words, 'God, have mercy on me, a sinner' (Luke 18:13). That prayer opens the way not only to heaven at the end of this earthly journey, but opens the way to heaven on earth – enjoying the possibilities of prayer.

But there is one other thing prayer does for God: we please him by our faith. Without faith it is impossible to do this. Those who come to God must believe not only that he exists, but that he rewards those who seek him (Heb. 11:6). Nothing gives God greater pleasure than getting to reward those who seek him.

Yes, God *can* work in us apart from prayer. Let us never – ever – forget that. He is sovereign and works all things according to the counsel of his will (Eph. 1:11). Our very seeking the Lord is because his Spirit was *already* at work in us. In other words, when I pray, especially when I am struggling, I may *feel* that the whole matter is entirely in my strength – and often I think I am getting nowhere! But when I keep on asking, diligently seeking him, I eventually come to realise that the Holy Spirit was graciously at the bottom of it all.

On the other hand, I love to quote John Wesley's viewpoint – namely, that God does nothing but in answer to prayer. I am not sure that is entirely true, because many times God *does* work apart from prayer. But Wesley's point is worth pondering; I myself take it very seriously and it has set me free to pray more than ever, ask more than ever, and expect more than ever.

In June 2002 I was met at the Tel Aviv airport by a Palestinian named Osama who drove me to my hotel in Jerusalem. Noting his name, I said to him, 'I pray for Osama bin Laden every day.' 'But why?' he asked. 'He is such an evil man.' 'That God would save him,' I replied. I told him that John Wesley taught that God does nothing but in answer to prayer. 'If that is true,' I continued, 'someone must have been praying for Saul of Tarsus, a terrorist if ever there was one.'

God has not yet answered my prayer regarding Osama bin Laden. God does not answer every prayer. Why? You tell me. I only know that I will keep asking for *everything* that is on my heart – until God says a definite, undeniable and irrefutable 'no'. Until then, whether pertaining to bin Laden, or my prayer for true revival in the Church – or anything else on my prayer list – I will continue to pour out my heart to God. Because, just maybe, what is on my heart is also on his heart.

In a word: prayer moves God's heart. I will not give up praying what is on my heart because I will choose to believe it is also on his heart. In that case, it is his heart moving us to pray.

2

What Prayer Does for Others

On him we have set our hope that he will
continue to deliver us, as you help us by your
prayers. Then many will give thanks on our
behalf for the gracious favour granted us in
answer to the prayers of many.

(2 Cor. 1:10–11)

Prayer can be generally defined as *asking God to act*.
Unless it is centred on worship, thanksgiving and
praise, prayer is essentially of two kinds: (1) when we pray
for ourselves, and (2) when we pray for others. The latter is
called intercession, when we plead on behalf of another.
It is what Jesus continually does for us (Heb. 7:25;
Rom. 8:34), and it is also what the Holy Spirit constantly
does for us (Rom. 8:26–27).

Praise, thanksgiving and worship have this in common

with intercession: it is 'unselfish praying' since the focus is not on ourselves. When we embark upon the ministry of interceding for another, we become truly selfless. One of the greatest things you can do for another person is to pray for him or her – or for a nation, the unsaved, the Church, an organisation, family, friend or enemy.

There are basically three kinds of unselfish praying: (1) praying for others, (2) praising God (called a sacrifice – Heb. 13:15), and (3) remembering to be *thankful*. One of the greatest verses in the Bible regarding prayer is Philippians 4:6, which even implies two kinds of praying, but adds the timely caution to be grateful:

> *Do not be anxious about anything, but in everything, by prayer and petition, with thanksgiving, present your requests to God.*

But remembering to be thankful – right and biblical though it is – could be carried out merely to be *heard* by God when we pray. There is nothing terribly wrong with that – after all, it is what we are told to do. I simply think we need to be as objective about ourselves as possible and be aware of our truest motives when we pray. As giving to the Lord *can* be done with a selfish motive – knowing we 'cannot out-give God' (2 Cor. 9:6–11) and hoping for something in return – it is also true that we cannot 'out-thank' the Lord. It is hard not to be aware of this when we pause to thank God for things and put our requests to him.

Two Greek words for prayer

Philippians 4:6 mentions two words: translated as 'prayer' (Greek: *proseuche*) and 'petition' (Greek: *deesei*). These two words can be used interchangeably and are often both translated as 'prayer'. But *deesei*, translated 'petition' ('supplication' – AV), is on occasions used with the more earnest kind of praying and is sometimes used to mean 'intercession'. For example, 'Brothers, my heart's desire and prayer [Greek: *deesis*] to God for the Israelites is that they may be saved.' This is a reference to Paul interceding on behalf of Israel. Nothing mattered more to Paul than the salvation of Israel, so he used *deesei* in this instance, which shows a deeper yearning and wish. This word is found in Luke 2:37 where it is used alongside fasting. It referred to Anna, a prophetess, who at the age of eighty-four worshipped night and day with 'fasting and praying' (Greek: *deesein*).

However, the slight difference in the two Greek words for prayer must not be pushed too far. They both can be translated as 'prayer' – that is, 'asking' or 'requesting'.

But when *asking God to act* is carried out on behalf of *others* we are lifted into the Big Leagues – we enter into intercession not unlike that of our Lord Jesus and of the Holy Spirit. It is an unselfish enterprise that brings great glory to God and does incalculable good for others.

So what does such praying do for others? It sets God into action on their behalf.

Consider what it did for Peter in the days of the early Church. When King Herod noticed how much it pleased the Jews when he beheaded James, the brother of John, he decided to arrest Peter and put him in prison. The thought of having to cope without Peter was unthinkable for the early Church, and they had not counted on such evil from King Herod. It certainly moved them to pray:

So Peter was kept in prison, but the church was earnestly praying to God for him. (Acts 12:5)

The Authorised Version says 'prayer was made without ceasing of the church unto God for him'. Here are some other versions: 'But earnest prayer was going up to God from the Church for his safety all the time he was in prison' (Living Bible); 'Peter was closely guarded in the prison, while the Church prayed to God earnestly on his behalf' (Phillips Modern English); 'All the time Peter was under guard the Church prayed to God for him unremittingly' (Jerusalem Bible); 'So Peter was kept in prison under constant watch, while the church kept praying fervently for him to God' (New English Bible).

There are no doubt two kinds of intercession: (1) perfunctory intercession, and (2) earnest intercession. The first kind is what often happens with so many of us when we are given a prayer list. We have all done this – praying rather perfunctorily – whether in public prayer meetings or at home. By 'perfunctory' I do not mean that one is unconcerned; I am simply pointing out that sometimes we pray through a list, interceding for those in need, but not with a burden of 'life or death' fervency.

But in the case of the earnest intercession of those in the early Church for Peter, their burden was so intense that it could not have been calculated. No adverb or adjective could even come close – 'earnest', 'unremittingly', 'tearfully', 'heartfelt', 'desperately' – to how they truly felt. The possibility of losing Peter was such an awful thought that they all prayed with a burden and concentrated intercession, such that no greater prayer can be imagined. It is the way that you and I would pray for a loved one who was in a critical condition.

And yet do not underestimate the power or effectiveness of what I have called 'perfunctory' intercession. Such prayer may go on for months or even years, and God hears such intercession. We are told these prayers are bottled up in heaven (Rev. 8:3–4).

It is simply that no human being could carry on indefinitely with the kind of intercession that was done by the Church on behalf of Peter when he was first imprisoned. We are not physically capable of praying like this for very long. And I would add that, if you find yourself praying with that kind of earnestness, it is a good sign; victory is not far away. God will not let us go on and on and on with this kind of heartbreaking agony without some breakthrough. It says in Acts that God stepped in and Peter was set free in a miraculous fashion (Acts 12:6–10).

God might have done this *without* the Church's earnest intercessory prayer, but he didn't. If John Wesley is indeed right – that God does nothing but in answer to prayer – God did not choose to act on Peter's behalf until the Church prayed as they did.

I doubt there is a greater mystery in the Bible than the subject of prayer. But the old saying 'Prayer changes things' is true – prayer makes things happen. So when you ask God to act for others, you are doing them a favour that cannot be measured here below.

Telling people that you pray for them

This is a hard question – should you tell people that you are praying for them, or do you simply tell God (and not let the people concerned know)? Let me explain why this is a hard question. If I tell you that I pray for you every day, this would undoubtedly encourage you. But what is my motive in telling you? Is it to make you think more of me – or is it to bless you? On balance, I would come down on the side of telling people you pray for them. When my friend Josef Tson was told by Dr Martyn Lloyd-Jones that he and his wife had prayed for Josef every day for the previous two or three years, Josef was overwhelmed. Dr Lloyd-Jones did not tell Josef this for any reason other than to encourage Josef – and it certainly did that.

When people tell us they pray for us it affirms us. It

makes us think that we must matter to others, and makes us feel good. So, yes, when you pray for others, tell them — so long as you don't do it to 'score points'! Our self-righteousness can nullify any good we hoped to accomplish within seconds.

However, I have made it a point (and I risk violating the very principle I am elaborating by telling *you* now!) to have a prayer list of people who will almost certainly never know that I pray for them every day. In some cases it was a temptation to tell them, but I have regarded it as a matter of discipline to keep some things private between God and me.

To put it another way: if I tell people I pray for them, my reward will very possibly be meted out only here below and not in heaven. This is because it would be forfeiting the honour I might have had from God alone had I not told them. But if I reckon that the encouragement I can give them by telling them I pray for them is truly uplifting to them, it is a reward in heaven I will willingly forfeit.

The Pharisees prayed only to be seen doing so (Matt. 6:5–6), and Jesus remarked that all that they did was 'done for men to see' (Matt. 23:5). If this is our motive, then it is clearly wrong to tell people we pray for them. But we can push the fear of being like the Pharisees a little bit too far; therefore, to reiterate, I think on balance it is good to tell people that you pray for them.

Paul is my biblical example for believing it is OK to tell people we are praying for them. To the church at Rome he stated that he remembered them in his 'prayers at all times' (Rom. 1:9–10); to the Ephesians, 'I keep asking that the God of our Lord Jesus Christ, the glorious Father, may give you the Spirit of wisdom and revelation, so that you may know him better' (Eph. 1:17); to the Philippians, 'In all my prayers for all of you, I always pray with joy' (Phil. 1:4); to the Colossians, 'Since the day we heard about you, we have not stopped praying for you' (Col. 1:9); to the church of the Thessalonians, 'We always thank God for all of you, mentioning you in our prayers' (1 Thess. 1:2). What an encouragement it must have been for Timothy to receive these words, 'Night and day I constantly remember you in my prayers. Recalling your tears' (2 Tim. 1:3–4). The same would be true of Philemon, 'I remember you in my prayers' (Philemon 4).

What does prayer do for others? The answer is two things: (1) it encourages them (if we tell them), and (2) it sets God into action on their behalf.

3

What Prayer Does for Us

Call to me and I will answer you and tell
you great and unsearchable things you
do not know. (Jer. 33:3)

Possibly the greatest fringe benefit of being a Christian is the privilege of prayer. I call it a 'fringe benefit' because it is not part of the package (that I know of) when the opportunity to become a Christian is presented. In other words, one is not told, 'Here is a good reason to become a Christian: you will be given the privilege of prayer.' I see nothing wrong if this were said to someone, but it is not what is normally put to a person before he or she comes to Christ. Prayer is, however, what you certainly discover on the first day of being a Christian!

By the way, if prayer is a *fringe* benefit, it is good to remind ourselves of certain things by posing the following

21

question: what is the *main* benefit of being a Christian? It is easy to take some essential things for granted, and I don't want to move on in this book without making clear what is the most important thing of all. I fear sometimes that people have forgotten this – some may even be offended by it. The main thing about being a Christian is that *you will go to heaven when you die because Jesus died on the cross for your sins*. This is the main reason he died. For your sins – not for healing, not for prosperity, not even so you can pray.

The stigma of the Christian faith

It is fashionable nowadays to say, 'If there were no heaven or no hell, I would still be a Christian.' Although I know what people mean by this, I must tell you as lovingly as I know how that the Apostle Paul would be horrified at this thought! He said the very opposite: 'If only for this life we have hope in Christ, we are to be pitied more than all men' (1 Cor. 15:19); 'If our hope in Christ is good for this life only, and no more, then we deserve more pity than anyone else in all the world' (Today's English Version); 'If our hope in Christ has been for this life only, we are the most unfortunate of all people' (Jerusalem Bible). And yet the Christian faith is too often presented as being something that exists mainly for us in the here and now. People seem not to want to face the fact that the Christian faith has been designed for us because we are a dying people and the wages of sin is death (Rom. 6:23). If there really is a heaven and there really is a hell, and when you consider that eternity lasts a long time, nothing is more important than eternal values.

To put it another way, there is an inherent stigma in the Christian faith. Caution: never, never, never try to outgrow the stigma (offence of the cross). It offends the sophisticated person to hear that the main thing about the gospel is that it fits us for heaven. I don't mean to be unfair, but I sometimes fear that there is a subtle, perhaps unconscious, attempt by some to de-stigmatise the gospel. This is a big mistake. It is like trying to get a car to run without fuel, or expect a bird to fly without wings, or fish to swim out of water. Paul knew he was on safe ground with the Galatians because of the *stigma* of the gospel he was upholding. What helps to prove that the gospel one preaches is the true gospel is that it *offends* (Gal. 5:11; 6:12–13); and de-stigmatising the gospel seeks to remove the offence of the cross.

Furthermore, you cannot appreciate prayer very much until you get to know the God of the Bible. And knowing the God of the Bible will bring you face to face with what I have just said about the gospel.

What, then, makes prayer the greatest fringe benefit of being a Christian?

*Why is prayer the greatest fringe benefit
of being a Christian?*

1 *Access to Supreme Power.* When you have access to the
true God you are in touch with the One who can make
things happen. An elementary teaching about God is that
he can do anything: 'For nothing is impossible with God'
(Luke 1:37); 'Ah, Sovereign LORD, you have made the
heavens and the earth by your great power and out-
stretched arm. Nothing is too hard for you' (Jer. 32:17); 'I
am the LORD, the God of all mankind. Is anything too hard
for me?' (Jer. 32:27)

'Life is not fair,' President John F. Kennedy used to say,
and one of the things that make life seem so unfair is that
only a minority have access to those who can make things
happen. Very few people have access to the president, the
prime minister, to a judge, to royalty, to those whose word
can change or influence so many things.

Let us say that you, for example, were not brought up in
a prestigious family. You did not have the best food, best
medical treatment, best clothes, best education or opportunities. If this sounds familiar, it is something I have in
common with you. My father earned just $8 a day when I
first went to school. I had never eaten a steak until I went
to university – when somebody took me out to a nice
restaurant. I got new shoes once a year – the day before
Easter. My education was inferior to those brought up in
other states. 'Thank God for Arkansas' was a slogan we

had in Kentucky, as I grew up in the days when there were only forty-eight states in America. Kentucky was *forty-seventh* in educational standards. I could go on and on. I will only say that I grew up with a severe inferiority complex, never mixed with the popular crowd at school, and being a Nazarene (called 'Noisyrenes' by those who scoffed at our freedom of worship) did not exactly help to get your name on to the society page of our local newspaper.

But regardless of whether you were brought up in poverty, or shunned by society, or feel powerless, it means nothing when it comes to Christianity. Being a Christian means access to God – the *only* Person with ultimate power. When asked why he wanted to be president of the United States, John F. Kennedy replied, 'Because that is where the power is.'

When it comes to God, we are *all* on level ground. Whether you are middle class, aristocratic, royal, rich, poor, red, yellow, black or white, you are valued by your heavenly Father as much as *anybody who has ever lived*. God will take on your case as if you are the most important person who has ever lived. Prayer gives you that privilege – access to ultimate power.

This is because God can make *anything* happen: he can heal; solve any problem; change your financial situation; vindicate you; open doors; cause everything that has happened in your past (whether it was right or wrong, or whether *you* were right or wrong) *work together for good*

(Rom. 8:28); find your friends; recognise your gift; use you as you are. That's what God does. That's part of his 'job description' if you will allow me to put it like that!

Prayer, then, gives you access to this God. He loves you as much as he loved Moses, Abraham, Joseph, the Apostle Paul – or Jesus. No good thing will he withhold from those who love him, fear him and want to please him (Ps. 84:11).

In a word: being a Christian transcends your background, culture, ability or inability, social or political status – and gives you access to the God of the Bible. He is your Creator and Redeemer. He knows your background backwards and forwards, knows your thoughts before you even have them, loves you with all your faults, knows the number of hairs on your head and . . . had you in mind when he created the world (see Ps. 139). And you, by prayer, have access to the King of kings and Lord of lords. Never, ever underestimate it. Never, ever, think that this may be true of others but not you – that's the devil speaking! Nobody is more important to God than you, dear reader – and I would go to the stake for this belief.

You – just as you are – have access to a greater power than can be conceived here on earth. Yes, *you*. You and I have this access because we are children of God. That is why prayer is the greatest fringe benefit of being a Christian.

2 *Prayer helps us to get to know the true God.* I come now to what I would regard as the most important thing

prayer does for us: it helps us to get to know the true God. Does this surprise you?

As I have just shown, getting to know the true God is not the only thing that prayer does for us, and perhaps you wanted me to say more about access to power. So what I now write is *not* what may excite you most of all. It may take time before you appreciate this, but the most important thing prayer does for us is to help us to get to know the true God. I would understand if you said that there are other things about prayer that mean more to you than that, but you will eventually come to see that the greatest thing prayer does for us is help us get to know personally the God of the Bible.

I had a surprising awakening not long ago when I was reading Exodus 33:13, which shows Moses' first reaction to the knowledge that he had found favour with God – a verse I have read a thousand times, but had not really grasped: 'If you are pleased with me, teach me your ways.' When I saw what this was saying, I was shaken rigid.

Think about this for a moment, and put yourself in Moses' shoes. Moses is handed on a silver platter a knowledge that is more extraordinary than any knowledge that could be wished for here below – namely, that God was pleased with him. I have to tell you, it doesn't get better than that! Exodus 33:13 tells us how Moses handled this sublime information: 'If you, Lord, are truly pleased with me, teach me your ways.'

Would you have responded that way? Would I? I doubt it,

I am ashamed to say. I have asked myself, if God said that to me – that he is pleased with me – and I could consequently ask for anything, what would I ask for?

I began asking friends this same question: 'If God said he was pleased with you and that you could now ask for *anything*, what would you ask him to do for you?' One friend said, 'That my daughter would come back to the Lord.' That is a good request, very understandable. Another said, 'That I would have good health.' Fair enough.

Another (who is not a Christian), said, 'That I could win the Lottery.' Another commented, 'That I would live a long life and be prosperous.' Jesus asked a blind man, 'What do you want me to do for you?' He replied, 'Lord, I want to see' (Luke 18:41).

What was it Moses asked for? He did not hesitate: 'If you are pleased with me, *teach me your ways*.' That immediate reply convicted me no end. I would like to think this would have been the answer I would have given, but I doubt it. But that is not all; Moses asked for this, '*so I may know you and continue to find favour with you*' (Exod. 33:13). Moses' request absolutely sobered me. I don't honestly think I would have asked for that. I would probably have asked for a greater anointing – which, you might say, is a spiritual request. Perhaps you are right – but Moses' reply shows how well he knew God already, and my own wish suggests I have a long way to go.

The most important thing prayer does for us, then, is to help us to know God and his *ways*.

God lamented of ancient Israel, 'They have not known my *ways*' (emphasis mine, Heb. 3:10; Ps. 95:10). When you get to know a person you learn that person's *ways*, what he or she is really like. My wife knows my ways – she usually knows whether I will like a particular film, TV programme, book or person. She often knows how I will answer most questions put to me. The main reason Louise knows my ways is because of the amount of time we have spent together – we know *each other*'s ways.

God wants *you* to know his ways. 'He made known his *ways* to Moses' (emphasis mine, Ps. 103:7). 'Be very careful to keep the commandment and the law that Moses the servant of the LORD gave you: to love the LORD your God, to walk in all his *ways*' (emphasis mine, Josh. 22:5). ' "My thoughts are not your thoughts, neither are your ways *my ways*," declares the LORD. "As the heavens are higher than the earth, so are *my ways* higher than your ways and my thoughts than your thoughts" ' (emphasis mine, Isa. 55:8–9).

When you spend time with a person, you get to know that individual. You can even read a person's books and feel that, to a degree, you get to know the author. I know I used to feel that way about Dr Martyn Lloyd-Jones – that I knew him a little because I read so much of what he wrote. I never dreamed that a day would come when I would get to spend a lot of time with him. During the last four years of his life I spent no fewer than two hours with him almost every Thursday in his home. What a privilege it was; I got to know his ways, his likes and dislikes, a bit about how his mind worked, how he would react to this or that. I reached a point where I knew instinctively what he would say about this person or that verse of Scripture, or that practice in a church. But I had an advantage over most people as very few got to know him, got to know his ways.

Time spent with God will open up his ways. Reading books won't do it. Reading theology won't do it. Studying creation won't do it. Going to church won't do it. Listening to religious music won't do it. Listening to great preaching won't do it. Even worshipping through hymns and choruses won't do it.

Liturgy – another word for written prayers – has its place in our spiritual development, and I love to read and pray the prayers of the great saints in church history. My wife Louise has compiled a book of great Christian prayers, one for every day of the year (*Great Christian Prayers*, Hodder & Stoughton). But reading these prayers each day will not *take the place of* spending time with the Lord.

But is there a danger of becoming legalistic with regard to the time spent in prayer each day? Yes, of course there is. You can also become so self-righteous that you drive too hard those people who live with you. You could (if you are not careful) also find yourself pointing the finger at those who don't pray as much as you do. I don't mean to sound critical, but this attitude would show that you have not really got to know the Lord very well after all. Knowing

God's ways *truly* will convict you of self-righteousness and pointing the finger.

There are days – sometimes several in a row – when I don't manage to pray as much as I like to, but I refuse to let this bother me. When my schedule settles down again, I make an attempt to return to what I think is a good habit – a decent amount of time spent with the Lord each day.

Only you can decide what that amount of time is. I have hinted already at what I think is right, depending on whether you are a church leader or layman.

You cannot 'out-give' the Lord when it comes to your money and God's work (he will bless you more than ever), you cannot 'out-thank' the Lord for his goodness (he will pour out more good things than ever), neither can you spend too much time with him. The more time I give to the Lord in quiet time or personal devotions, the more time I have for myself.

I realise that this type of guidance can play into the whims of some particular personalities. I knew of one lady in South Carolina who was known for being lazy and not keeping a tidy home – but who spent hours and hours every day in prayer. When it came to mealtimes, she was happy to sit down at the table, but when it came to washing the dishes she would say, 'I feel led to pray.' Everybody who knew her could see through this!

You can seek the Lord without spending a specific amount of time in prayer. Yes, seeking the Lord can be a lifestyle and a condition of the heart, but I commend to you the importance of waiting before the Lord – just with your Bible and perhaps a note pad. Make it something you do as regularly and as often as you can. You will see the difference and will thank God for every minute you have given him. I promise it.

3 *Prayer will keep changing your life.* The Christian faith launches someone on a new journey, and this is because you have been given a new life. You have been 'born again' – by the Holy Spirit (John 3:3–7). But God does not say to you at your conversion, 'Nice to meet you – see you in heaven.' No. It is the beginning not only of a relationship with him, but of an *ongoing* changing of your life.

Paul calls it being changed from 'glory to glory', which means being transformed into Christ's image 'from one degree of glory to another' (2 Cor. 3:18 – English Standard Version). It is being renewed again – and again – to repentance, which means that our minds are continually being changed. Repentance (Greek: *metanoia*) means 'change of mind', so as we get to know God we get to know ourselves. Like a loving, wise parent who does not tell us all he or she knows, so our heavenly Father – who sees our flaws and defects long before he lets us see them – patiently leads each of us by the hand one day at a time.

It is through prayer that the Bible comes alive and we are given to see not only insights into Holy Scripture but also into ourselves. I am seventy-two as I write, and I would blush to tell you how much changing I still have to do. It is embarrassingly wonderful! My first reaction is, 'Lord, why didn't you show me this before?' or 'Lord, how could you keep loving me so much when you knew all the time what horrible faults I have?'

When I retired from Westminster Chapel in 2002 at the age of sixty-six, I was not prepared for how much I would learn about God and myself in what are supposed to be my 'retirement' years.

In other words, we never stop learning and we never stop growing.

But this ongoing changing of mind, heart, will and life are not likely to happen other than through faithful prayer. When Louise and I first came back to America I wondered if, perhaps, I would not pray as much as I did when I was the minister of Westminster Chapel. I thought, 'I don't need to prepare new sermons, I can preach old ones, I won't need to pray as much.' I can tell you, after *one week* of praying somewhat less than I had been doing, I felt the difference. I had no idea how much I would miss my regular time of prayer. So I returned to the exact pattern of prayer I had followed all those years in London – and I am all the better for it.

At the risk of making you think I am very spiritual (and, maybe, forfeiting any reward in heaven), I must tell you that in fact I pray as much, if not more, than ever. If you think that I have more time now that I am 'retired', I have to tell you that I am far busier these days than when I was the pastor of Westminster Chapel. I preach more than ever, write more than ever, and travel at what to me feels like a very punishing schedule. But I pray as much as ever.

Because I am not a nocturnal type (I begin to turn into a cabbage around 9 p.m.!), I love to wait before God at the beginning of each day, thinking 'what will he show me today?' The anticipation is as great as ever and I would not miss it for the world. I see not only things I need to learn about myself (changes in my attitudes – towards my wife and family, and others), but points in Scripture I had not seen before.

It just gets better and better.

But this is not so *every* day. Some days I have to work at it, perhaps because I did not sleep as well the night before, perhaps because I am preoccupied with a problem, or – and this happens often – because God is hiding his face from me. That means I feel *nothing* when I pray: no insights come, no sense of his presence, a complete absence of clear thinking. This can last for days or weeks. This is why Paul cautioned us to be 'instant' 'in season' (when you feel God's presence) and 'out of season' (2 Tim. 4:2) – that is, when he hides his face. It is worth noting that this word came in what is generally regarded to be Paul's final epistle before he died, meaning that the aged and mature Paul still experienced the hiding of God's face.

Does this mean we don't need to bother to pray when God hides his face? Do we seek him only when it feels good? No!

I would therefore urge you to spend as much time in

prayer as you can, for, without it, the changing you need will be minimised. It is through prayer – time with God – that you get to know his *ways*, plus those things that you need to know about yourself. God *could* change you apart from prayer, but he probably won't. He likes your company, and the reward for spending as much time with him as you possibly can is greater than you can imagine.

Never forget this – there will be no praying in heaven. Do it now, and be changed. People will like you more; you will like yourself more; you will like others more; you will like prayer more; you will love the Bible more. I guarantee it.

But now let us turn to some practical things – such as how you actually spend that time in prayer.

PART TWO

The Bible, The Holy Spirit
And Prayer

4

Why Read the Bible?

But the Counsellor, the Holy Spirit . . . will
remind you of everything I have said to you.

(John 14:26)

Prayer and Bible reading go together. They should be inseparable, just as the Word and Spirit should be. I regard time reading the Scriptures as a vital and necessary part of one's private devotional life. If, say, a person sets aside thirty minutes a day to pray, I do not assume that one is *only praying* for that time. It should also include reading your Bible – I recommend at least a chapter a day.

Dr Martyn Lloyd-Jones recommended a Bible-reading plan designed by the saintly Scottish preacher Robert Murray M'Cheyne (1813–43). It takes a person through the whole Bible in a year, including the New Testament and Psalms twice. But it is a bit rigorous for many Christians, although a good number of our members followed it faithfully when I was at Westminster Chapel. I have turned to a Bible-in-a-year plan more recently, just for a change, although I may well go back to M'Cheyne's plan at some point.

The significant thing about a good Bible reading plan is that it (1) keeps you in the Word daily, and (2) enables you to read through the entire Bible over a reasonable period of time. I have discovered that there are many people who have been in Christian service all their lives, but have not read the Bible all the way through. This is sad.

As far back as I can remember, certainly from my teenage years, I read from the Bible every day – but with no plan for a long time. Although I knew my Bible quite well, I would have known it even better had I followed a plan that told me where to read, day by day. My wife Louise has her own plan – she had come up with it before we married, and it has served her well. She knows her Bible backwards and forwards, possibly better than I do.

I cannot over-stress how much God wants his people to read his Word because the Bible is God's integrity put on the line.

I don't know who expressed the following for the first time, but the reasoning behind it goes something like this: if you do nothing but read your Bible you will *dry up*, if you only pray you will *blow up*, but if you read your Bible *and* pray you will *grow up*. There is a lot of truth to this, but I also think more is needed than this. One needs to *experience* God.

I have cherished a prophetic word given to me many years ago by Alex Buchanan. He said, 'R.T., you must not only convey the Word when you preach, but you must convey *God himself*.' I knew exactly what he meant and that he was right. I needed that. It was not enough that I was sound in my teaching. The question was whether my people were experiencing *God* when I preached. I sought from that moment to make that my goal, not theological soundness.

This should happen when we pray; we should experience God. This is why both Bible reading and prayer go together.

One of the burdens of my heart in recent years has been the need to bring the Word and Spirit together. In the early Church there was no separation between the two: 'Our gospel came to you not simply with words, but *also with power*, with the Holy Spirit' (emphasis mine, 1 Thess. 1:5).

I take the view that there has largely been a silent divorce in the Church between the Word and the Spirit. You have those who are immediately recognisable as being on the 'Word' side – emphasising doctrine, expository preaching and the theology of men like Luther, Calvin and Jonathan Edwards. You also have those whose emphasis is instantly noticeable by their stress on signs and wonders, gifts of the Spirit, lively worship, and the need to get back to what was commonplace in the Book of Acts.

Both emphases are exactly right, but so often you

cannot get 'Word' people to see their lack of fondness for the immediate coming down of the Spirit, and sometimes you cannot get 'Spirit' people to see the need for theological excellence. It is *both* that are needed desperately at the present time, and the simultaneous combination will, I believe, eventually result in spontaneous combustion – and we will be back in the Book of Acts! And Romans!

In the meantime our private devotional lives should be the combination of prayer and Bible reading that will bring us right into the presence of God. But by 'presence of God' I really mean his *manifest* presence – God himself is always present of course, being omnipresent. But it is the conscious, experienced presence that you and I need to feel when we are alone with God. Yes, *feel*. Don't be afraid of that word. We are all emotional beings and we love feeling happy and joyful. That is what we should experience in God's presence.

I mentioned Robert Murray M'Cheyne above. He became a legend largely because of the genuine revival that broke out in his church in Dundee, Scotland. The article about him in *The New International Dictionary of the Christian Church* (Paternoster) says that the fruitfulness of his ministry and his own spiritual growth 'were the outcome of a strict daily programme of Bible study, prayer, meditation' alongside his pastoral duties. Many of us recoil at the thought of a strict plan of daily Bible reading and prayer, but where has the freedom from such strictness got us? Personally, I need a regular plan – or I fear lapsing into little or no time with God. I know this because I have lapsed too often.

At any rate, praying and reading our Bibles should be done in a manner that is not merely cerebral. Those of us on the 'Word' side tend to be intellectual and verbal, emphasising knowledge. Those of us on the 'Spirit' side tend to be more non-verbal, focusing on what is heart-felt. As Bible reading and prayer are inseparable, and as we need the Word joined with the Spirit, so too must our private devotional lives be bent on both clear thinking and a heart-felt seeking after God.

I said above that the Bible is God's integrity put on the line. He bares himself by giving us his written Word. The Bible is made up of sixty-six books, thirty-nine in the Old Testament, twenty-seven in the new – written over a period of 3,000 years. Jesus divided the Old Testament into three parts: (1) the Law of Moses (the first five books of the Old Testament), (2) the Prophets – which would include both the historical books (e.g. Joshua, 1 and 2 Samuel, 1 and 2 Kings, 1 and 2 Chronicles) and the canonical prophets from Isaiah to Malachi, and (3) the Psalms (which possibly includes the wisdom literature as in Proverbs and Ecclesiastes). God used men whose personalities and cultures came through in what they wrote. And yet what is recorded in the Bible was God-breathed – inspired of God because men *spoke from God* 'as they were carried along by the Holy Spirit' (1 Tim. 3:16; 2 Pet. 1:21).

The Bible is God's *revealed will*. The Puritans made a distinction between the secret will of God and his revealed will. The secret will pertains to the knowledge that he alone has of the future – who will be saved, what will happen, where you will be ten years from now. God knows the future as perfectly as he knows the past. But he does not reveal as much about the future as we may wish. However curious we may be about the secret will, it shows more devotion to God when you want to know his revealed will – the Bible.

A friend of mine who is known for his unusual prophetic gift told me about a lady who came up to him and said, 'Do you have a word for me?' This was (it felt to him) the thousandth person to ask the same question of him that day, and to his regret he actually got annoyed, saying, 'YES – here, take this' (handing her his Bible). She took it as a *rhema* word – from God himself. When my friend was in the area a couple of years later, that same woman had read and re-read the Bible, knowing it better than the ministers in the area! She had become immersed not in the secret will of God, but in his revealed will.

When we care to know God well enough to read his Word, line by line, day by day – out of love for him – it pleases him more than nearly anything we can do. This is how we know his *ways*. The funny thing is that the more we seek to know him through his revealed will, the better we often know his secret will (e.g. Should I do this? Should

I do that? Take this job? Marry this person?). Because the more you are acquainted with his *ways* by reading his Word, the more you anticipate exactly what he would tell you – as by a prophetic word.

Some Christians love a prophetic word (especially if it tells them what they like to hear) or an extraordinary word of knowledge, sometimes called the *rhema* Word – a direct word for the immediate situation. But the more you know the revealed will of God, the more likely you are to get the occasional *rhema* Word. It is not a sign of a good spiritual appetite to live entirely for a *rhema* Word. It is rather like living on fast food all the time – akin to those who prefer a quick snack rather than a meal because they are always in a hurry.

Carefully reading the Bible, at least a chapter a day, seven days a week, is an indication of how much you esteem God.

Let me give you what I regard as one of the best reasons to read the Bible. Jesus promised that when the Holy Spirit came he would remind us of what we had been taught: 'But the Counsellor, the Holy Spirit, whom the Father will send in my name, will teach you all things and will remind you of everything I have said to you' (John 14:26). Think about it. The disciples heard Jesus teach so much. They heard the Sermon on the Mount, they heard the parables, they heard his applications, they heard his replies to the Pharisees. 'How can I remember these things?' they must have thought. Jesus said in so many words: 'Not to worry.

The Holy Spirit will bring to your remembrance what I have taught.' And he did!

So with you. Perhaps reading the Bible is not always inspirational. There are times ('in season') when the Bible comes alive, and there are times ('out of season') when it seems boring. This is why Paul said to be prepared 'in season and out of season' (2 Tim. 4:2). Why? Because the Holy Spirit will suddenly remind you of what you have read! You felt nothing at the time, but later on the Holy Spirit comes alongside and reminds you of what you thought you had forgotten!

Let me put it another way. If the Spirit of God comes down on the Church (as I pray for and believe), who will he use? What servants of Christ will be his sovereign instruments in a time of genuine revival? I answer: those who took the time to read, listen to teaching, and learn when it seemed so uninteresting. That's who! I don't mean to be unfair, but if you are empty-headed before the Spirit comes down, you will be empty-headed afterwards!

So why should you read the Bible? *So there will be something in your head for the Spirit to remind you of!*

The Bible is the Holy Spirit's greatest product. He inspired it and has not changed his mind on what he intended to say. We all like short-cuts in life, and sometimes we are in a hurry – wanting 'food' that is ready to eat without waiting. But if your desire is truly to please God, make a commitment *today* (if you haven't already) to get to know him by giving him a never-looking-back promise to know his Word, the Bible. Treat and read it in the same way as the woman who believed my prophetic friend so much that she took him seriously and read the Bible for her *rhema* Word!

subjects such as these

5

Being on Good Terms with the Bible's Author

Do not grieve the Holy Spirit of God, with
whom you were sealed for the day of
redemption. (Eph. 4:30)

In order to understand the Bible we need the help of its
Author, the Holy Spirit. One is never brought to Jesus
Christ in the first place without the effectual, supernatural
work of the Spirit (John 16:7).

Not only that – as a believer who expects to understand
the Bible, you must be on good terms with the
Holy Spirit. This would not be true with any other book.
You don't need the Holy Spirit to understand architecture,
anthropology, literature, history, philosophy, art,
algebra, physics, chemistry, medicine, science, music,
psychology, sociology, computer science – or even man-made
theology. This is because you can read and grasp
subjects such as these at the *natural* level.

But the Bible, being a spiritual book, is utterly and totally different. It was written by men, yes, but inspired, overruled and sealed by the Holy Spirit, and its deepest meaning can only be fully grasped at the *spiritual* level. You don't need the Holy Spirit to understand the arts and sciences – a good intellect will do. But without the Holy Spirit's guidance, the greatest intellect on the planet – the person with the highest IQ – will read the Bible over and over again and come short of the true and full interpretation of God's infallible Word. If he or she says, 'The Bible makes no sense,' that person will probably think it is down to their superior brain power, but that is not the reason that they don't understand it. Only the Holy Spirit can interpret his own Word. There is a profound line in William Cowper's great hymn 'God moves in a mysterious way his wonders to perform' which reads, 'God is his own interpreter and He will make it plain.'

Only God understands his own mind; only the Holy Spirit can interpret what he wrote when he moved on holy men of old to write the Bible.

It therefore requires a good relationship with the Holy Spirit if you intend to understand the Bible. It means to enjoy the *ungrieved* Holy Spirit, a phrase I will unfold below. I'm afraid it means *obedience* to God, the gospel, his Son's teaching and the commands set down in Holy Writ if you expect to understand the Bible. It means dealing with sin in your life – bitterness, jealousy, greed, lust, dishonesty, vengeance, holding grudges, all those things that grieve the Holy Spirit – if you want truly to understand the Bible.

This point cannot be emphasised strongly enough. Only the Holy Spirit can accurately interpret Scripture, so if you want to know the Bible you must know the Holy Spirit and his *ways*.

The problem is that the Holy Spirit is a very, very *sensitive* person. When we speak of another person as being 'very sensitive' it is not exactly a compliment. But, like it or not, that is the way the Holy Spirit is. You may want to say, 'He ought not to be that way – he should not be so sensitive.' I do understand, but this is the way he is and he is the only Holy Spirit we have! He is a person who can get his feelings hurt.

When Paul cautioned, 'And do not *grieve* the Holy Spirit of God, with whom you were sealed for the day of redemption' (emphasis mine, Eph. 4:30), he used a Greek word (Greek: *lupeite*, grieve) that means getting your feelings hurt. We hurt the feelings of the Holy Spirit, for example, when we refuse to forgive those who have hurt us.

Have you ever seen a person in grief? Have you ever been in a state of grief? It is not a pleasant feeling. And yet when I think that I am capable of bringing *grief* to the Holy Spirit, it makes me want to be careful not to do this. I do not want to cause the Holy Spirit to have any grief over my actions or attitudes.

A young minister in Alabama asked me, 'What does a veteran like you have in the way of advice for a young preacher like me?' I answered: find out what grieves the Holy Spirit and don't do it.

All Christians have the Holy Spirit (Rom. 8:9), but not all Christians enjoy the presence of the *ungrieved* Holy Spirit. When he is ungrieved – a wonderful condition to enjoy – it is like the Holy Spirit coming down on Jesus as a dove and *remaining* on him (John 1:32–33). I know what it is for the Dove to come down on me. It is absolutely wonderful. The peace, the joy, the feeling that all is under control. There is nothing quite like it. But my problem is that the Dove doesn't stay down long! Hours later I sense that something went wrong – I grieved him and he fluttered away. It may have been by a wrong attitude, speaking curtly to someone on the phone, getting angry in traffic. I'm sorry, but it doesn't take a lot to grieve him. He gets hurt easily.

I know of no greater challenge on earth than this: to find out what grieves the Spirit and also to *stop yourself* from grieving him when you are about to do it. You can catch yourself when you begin to know the Spirit's *ways*. When I find myself coming close to shouting at someone in traffic, telling a person off on the phone, repeating gossip, speaking abruptly to my wife, or refusing to forgive another person totally, but manage to *stop myself*, I can avoid the Dove flying away. I reckon that the Holy Spirit is depicted as a dove because the dove is a very shy bird.

A story I tell in *The Sensitivity of the Holy Spirit* is worth repeating here. A British couple, Sandy and Bernice, were sent by their denomination to Israel as missionaries and were placed in a home near Jerusalem. A few weeks later they noticed that a dove had come to live in the eaves of the roof of their home. They were so excited; it was like a seal of God on their being there. But they noticed that every time they slammed a door – or shouted at each other in an argument – the dove would fly away. One day Sandy said to Bernice, knowing how much both of them wanted to keep the dove around them, 'Either the dove adjusts to us – or we adjust to the dove.' It changed their lives, just to keep a bird nearby. And yet the Holy Spirit himself is a thousand times more sensitive than the dove.

Adjusting to the gentle, heavenly Dove means controlling our spirit, restraining our words, sorting out our wrong attitudes, being sure we are not bitter, and that we have totally forgiven those who have injured us in any way.

Here is the point. When the Spirit is *ungrieved* in us, we will have the presence of his mind – self-control. All the fruits of the Spirit flow to the degree he is not grieved by us: love, joy, peace, patience, kindness, goodness, faithfulness, gentleness, self-control (Gal. 5:22–23).

The bottom line is: when the Dove remains on us (which means the Spirit is ungrieved), we begin to qualify to understand the Bible.

What is more, it makes *all the difference* in our praying. That grieving of the Holy Spirit may occur in many ways. For example, this is why Peter said, 'Husbands . . . be considerate as you live with your wives . . . *so that nothing will hinder your prayers'* (emphasis mine, 1 Pet. 3:7). I myself can testify to this – over and over again. When I want to have a good time alone with the Lord – but am having an ongoing quarrel with my wife – my praying is null and void in so far as feeling any edification from prayer is concerned. I simply cannot feel angry towards Louise and enjoy communion with the Holy Spirit at the same time. It is impossible. In much the same way, I cannot read the Bible with understanding when I am angry – for whatever reason.

So if I am going to enjoy praying and reading the Bible I must be on good terms with the Holy Spirit.

When Jesus introduced the Holy Spirit to the Twelve, he said a number of things about the Spirit, including that (1) he is a person, (2) the Spirit would be, like Jesus, a Comforter – or Helper (John 14:16), (3) he would be the Spirit of truth (John 14:17), (4) he would be a teacher, (5) he would bring the teachings of Jesus to our remembrance (John 14:26), (6) he would guide us into all truth, and (7) he would show things to come (John 16:13). However, all that Jesus had to say about the Holy Spirit and our experience of him assumes that we have not grieved the Spirit. In other words, the promise of being guided into all truth and having the Spirit bring things to our remembrance assumes that we are on good terms with the Holy Spirit. It is quite wrong to assume that the Spirit will guide us into all truth, plus show us things to come, when we are angry with our brothers and sisters, and not honouring the teachings of Jesus and the Apostles.

I am quite sure that a person can be a good doctor, surgeon, dentist or lawyer without any knowledge of the Holy Spirit. It does not matter whether that person is faithful in marriage, committed to Jesus Christ in his personal life, or lives a life having totally forgiven one's enemies.

But not so with the Christian. You and I cannot get away with unholy living and then expect to enjoy intimate fellowship with the Father when we have time alone with God in prayer.

And since Bible and prayer go together, we are faced with this fact: we must respect the Holy Spirit in our public and private lives day and night, and we respect him by avoiding anything that might grieve him.

But when he is not grieved, we are in a very good position to hear him speak, whether through the Bible or *directly to us*.

Yes! The kind of relationship that people had in the days of the early Church can be ours today. One day, quite unexpectedly, Philip felt prompted to go in a certain direction, having no idea why or where it would lead (Acts 8:26). This was an immediate and direct witness of the Spirit, and that can happen today. As Dr Martyn Lloyd-Jones used to say to us again and again, 'The Bible was not given to replace the supernatural or miraculous; it was given to correct abuses.' And yet the more we know the

Bible, the more likely it is that we will experience the immediate and direct guidance of the Spirit – if he is ungrieved in us.

Prayer can be hard work and, as I said above, not always thrilling. In fact, it is often more about praying 'out of season' than praying 'in season'. There is no child of God – living or dead – who would tell you that prayer is always glorious and full of wonder and joy.

But when I know that God likes my company, that spurs me on to wait for him! And when the Holy Spirit is ungrieved in me, and I know when this is the case, I can cope with the dry seasons. Because I also know that *any minute* he might show up and reveal something to me or manifest his joy. He is like that, and loves to do it.

6

Praying without a Sense of God

*Truly you are a God who hides himself, O God
and Saviour of Israel. (Isa. 45:15)*

One of the best sermons I ever heard Richard Bewes
(former Rector at London's All Souls Church) preach
was at Westminster Chapel, a talk he called 'Between the
Times'. He described how so much of life is just that –
'between the times' – when things aren't apparently
'happening', whether referring to the lives of inventors,
composers or any number of creative people. Such people
do indeed have their high water marks when a breakthrough comes, but most of the time is about *waiting* for
such a moment. His sermon helped me no end.

This is because I too have found it precisely like that.
Most of life is 'between the times'. I once talked to a friend
whose father was a special agent with MI6. I asked him

what it was like when his father was doing dangerous stuff like you see in a tense James Bond film. He assured me that special intelligence work was 99 per cent boredom and drudgery. It was mostly waiting. And more waiting. It was, generally speaking, very *unexciting*. The James Bond films focus on the 'times' rather than 'between the times' – and that's what makes spy thrillers so exciting. Who would go to the cinema to watch a spy doing nothing but waiting and waiting for something to happen? But true life in that world is in fact like that – not a lot of fun.

I therefore do not want my book on prayer to give the wrong impression. My best times are when I pray. Yes, that is absolutely true. But I have to tell you also that some of my *worst times are when I pray*. My prayer life is more 'between the times' than times of breakthrough, discovery, insight, immediate and direct witness of the Spirit and an acute sense of the presence of God.

It is what Paul means by being faithful, consistent and prepared 'out of season' (2 Tim. 4:2). I regard that expression as one of Paul's most helpful and practical commands. Keep in mind that 2 Timothy was, almost certainly, Paul's very last epistle before he went to heaven. He wrote that letter to Timothy while he was waiting for his own execution in Rome. He exhorts Timothy to be 'prepared [*instant* – AV] in season *and* out of season'. One must be faithful with or without a sense of accomplishment and help from the Holy Spirit. Paul does not want to depart from this earth by giving Timothy the impression that Christian ministry is always accompanied by a great sense of the presence of God – in other words, when preaching or praying is happy and exciting.

'In season' is when God shows up. 'Out of season' is between the times – when you wait, and wait, and wait. It is when God hides his face. 'Truly you are a God who hides himself, O God and Saviour of Israel' (Isa. 45:15).

I write this chapter because I need to put you in the picture as fully as possible. I admit to having very wonderful times in prayer, but to be *equally* candid, I have to tell you I know what it is – so much of the time – to wait before the Lord with my Bible and note pad, and having to give up after an hour or two without any great feeling of joy or fresh insights. Most mornings (my favourite time to pray) are actually like this.

John Newton – famous largely for his hymn 'Amazing Grace' – actually wrote a hymn nearly every week when he was the rector of the parish church in Olney, Buckinghamshire. He would write a hymn that corresponded to the Sunday sermon. Not all his hymns became known, and possibly some of them were never sung twice. Many of them are quite mediocre. And yet his parishioners must have enjoyed his vulnerability. Going through my Olney Hymnal one day, I was a little surprised, but pleased, to find how John Newton in a hymn described times of dryness and wandering thoughts when *in prayer*. It is one thing to have unspiritual thoughts now and then, even to have them often. But in *prayer*? Yes.

In a virtually unknown hymn, 'Kindle, Saviour in my heart a flame of love divine', Newton not only described how he sometimes felt nothing when he prayed but also how his mind wandered and he had unspiritual thoughts. He summarised it like this:

> *Often at the mercy-seat, while calling on thy name,*
> *Swarms of evil thoughts I meet, which fill my soul*
>   *with shame,*
> *Agitated in my mind, like a feather in the air,*
> *Can I thus a blessing find? My soul, can this be*
>   *prayer?*

I have had similar thoughts more than I care to admit. I will only say that verse describes me. 'My soul, can this be prayer?' I too have found myself saying. I ask: 'How can I expect to be blessed when this is the best I can do in my quiet time?' And yet if the great, saintly John Newton could have thoughts like that, there must be hope for me!

In another hymn, a little better known, Newton wrote words that show how God answers prayer in a way that one does not particularly want. We used to sing this one at Westminster Chapel, although about once a year was enough – it is a bit intense. And yet I find this encouraging too:

> *I asked the Lord that I might grow*
> *In faith, and love, and every grace,*

Might more of His salvation know,
And seek more earnestly His face.

T'was He who taught me thus to pray,
And He, I trust, has answered prayer;
But it has been in such a way
That almost drove me to despair.

I hoped that in some favoured hour
At once He'd answer my request;
And, by His love's constraining power,
Subdue my sins, and give me rest.

Instead of this, He made me feel
The hidden evils of my heart,
And let the angry powers of hell
Assault my soul in every part.

'Lord, why is this?' I trembling cried,
'Wilt Thou pursue Thy worm to death?'
''Tis in this way', the Lord replied,
'I answered prayer for grace and faith'.

In a word: when we don't feel particularly spiritual, or don't enjoy God's manifest presence, he may still be powerfully at work in us.

Jackie Pullinger, the legendary servant of Christ who has worked with drug addicts in Hong Kong, told me how her ministry there 'took off'. She said she began praying in tongues for fifteen minutes a day – 'by the clock', she added. 'I felt *nothing*,' she went on to say, 'but that is when we began to see conversions.'

This goes to show that when God hides his face he only *appears* to hide his face. When there is no sense of his presence, it is down to our subjective feelings – not what is objectively true.

God holds back a sense of his presence many times when we pray, to test us – to see how much we persevere without that sense of his presence. It is easy to pray when we feel his presence; it is hard to pray without this. But either way *his presence is there* – whether we feel him with us or not.

I have a hunch that we please him most when we persevere in faith, pray, work and rely on him *without* a sense of his presence. When he allows us to feel his presence we may think we are pleasing him more. I rather think it is him pleasing *us* more in such times. I suspect we please *him* most when we continue on and, as Jackie Pullinger put it, we feel 'nothing'. 'And without faith it is impossible to please God, because anyone who comes to him must believe that he exists and that he rewards those who earnestly seek him' (Heb. 11:6).

What makes faith *faith* is that we continue to believe without tangible, empirical evidence that we have got it right. If we had the evidence that we naturally wanted, we wouldn't need faith! And yet, although the presence of God is not something we can call 'tangible' or 'empirical', it is quite true that if one experiences a great sense of his presence then less faith is needed – at that time. It is easier to believe when God is manifesting his presence powerfully.

For example, I know what it is like to feel God so near and to be so real that I find myself saying to him, 'Lord, how could I have ever doubted you? You are being so real right now, so near.' In other words, during the time God makes himself so real to us, it is not faith so much at work as it is feeling like a spectator – watching God work. There are times when he is, literally, so real that seeing him visibly would not make him more real. That is something that the immediate and direct witness of the Holy Spirit is capable of doing. Forgive me if you have heard this before from me, but I can never get over it. When the Lord unveiled his glory to me on 31 October 1955, while driving in my car, he was literally more real than anybody or anything in my sight. That lasted for a while, but not very long.

Those people described in Hebrews 11, the faith chapter of the Bible, had their high water marks. But the events that the writer of Hebrews chose to describe are those that were between the times. Noah built an ark at a time when there had been no rain. He must have felt a fool, and people must have laughed at him for seeming to be so ridiculous. But he pressed on, and when the rain came, drowning all the inhabitants on earth, Noah saved his family and became 'heir of the righteousness that comes by faith'.

Hebrews 11 was written to demonstrate *faith*, which is defined as being sure of what we hope for and certain of what 'we do not see' (Heb. 11:1). How can one be 'certain' of what you can't see? But that is just what makes faith, *faith*. Like it or not, God has decreed to bless those who live by faith, those who rely on his own Word.

The natural way to look at things is to say, 'Seeing is believing.' But it cannot be called *faith* when you see it and then believe it! Those who mocked Jesus at his crucifixion said, 'Let this Christ, this King of Israel, come down now from the cross, that we may *see and believe*' (emphasis mine, Mark 15:32). To them, seeing would have enabled them to believe, but such 'belief' is not dignified with the title of 'faith' when it is based on seeing first.

Faith, then, is being certain of what we do not see. Abraham was commanded to go to a place called an inheritance, 'even though he did not know where he was going' (Heb. 11:8). Moses chose to be 'ill-treated along with the people of God rather than to enjoy the pleasures of sin for a short time. He regarded disgrace for the sake of Christ as of greater value than the treasures of Egypt.' When you examine his life in the Book of Exodus you will see that he apparently felt nothing at the time – in so far as a sense of God's presence was concerned. Indeed, he was 'looking ahead to his reward' (Heb. 11:25–26). He knew he would be very glad indeed if he did not give up.

That is what prayer is often like. It is carried out by faith alone. It is faith only in Jesus' death on the cross that counts for righteousness in God's sight – even though you may feel nothing when you initially transfer your trust in your good works to his shed blood. It is likewise faith alone through the enterprise of prayer as you keep on relying on God's promise – when feeling nothing – that pleases God. Yes, God likes that. We are justified by faith (Rom. 4:5), and we also live by faith (Heb. 11).

Praying that pleases God is done mostly between the times. When it is out of season. When God seems to withdraw his presence and hide his face. Why? To let us see for ourselves how much he means to us. I might have said, 'To let God see for himself how much he means to us.' Yes, I could have said that. After all, when Abraham was willing to sacrifice his son Isaac, God said to Abraham, 'Now I know that you fear God, because you have not withheld from me your son, your only son' (Gen. 22:12). But that was language of accommodation. God was reaching Abraham on his level. The truth is that God knew that Abraham feared him, but Abraham needed to see for *himself* that he truly feared God.

In this same way, God requires things of us that do not make sense at the time. God gives us instructions that only show the step we need to take one day at a time. God lets us be tested to the hilt – but it is for us. We need to see for ourselves that we will not give up or give in. We may *think* we are showing him something he had not known until that moment, but the truth is that he sees the end from the beginning, he learns nothing from us. We are the ones who are learning.

And one of the most important things we learn is that

we persevere in the midst of trial and temptation in a manner – between the times – that reveals our love for him.

As I have shared with you, I know what it is to pray without any sense of God. It is not a time of inspiration. I know what it is to preach without any sense of God. Believe me, it ain't fun. I know what it is to pray inwardly as I struggle in preaching, 'God, please let me get this sermon over with so I can rush into the vestry and bow my head in shame for such poor, pitiful preaching' – only to learn later that someone was converted during the same sermon!

I know what it is to give out tracts on a bitterly cold Saturday morning in Buckingham Gate in London – with almost nobody accepting a tract or being willing to listen. And then returning home feeling I was a failure – only to learn months later that the one person who *did* accept a tract read it and was converted.

While preaching in Scotland recently I had a lady ask me to pray for her at the end of the service. I did, and felt nothing. I would have forgotten the incident had she not written two months later to remind me of it and to tell me that she too 'felt nothing' when I prayed. But four hours later, she wrote, the headache she had so acutely that day (and which had been her lot more or less continuously for five years) completely left her – and never came back.

Having preached on 'Totally forgiving ourselves' in an Anglican church in North London, I offered to pray for those who needed physical healing. I did this partly because holding a grudge towards others or towards ourselves can lead to serious illness and disease, and total forgiveness can result in physical healing. I prayed a general prayer for those who responded to my appeal and who remained at the front of the church – 'Be healed in Jesus' name'. That is all I said. I felt nothing. But as I was writing this chapter a lady wrote to say that a woman in that group, who was almost completely deaf in one ear and partially deaf in the other, was healed in both ears.

It is often true that when a real healing takes place through prayer, one feels nothing at the time (both the one who does the praying and the one who is prayed for), and it is only discovered later that healing started to take place.

We should be content in season, and also out of season. We should persevere in prayer when we are 'between the times' as well as when we feel a sense of God's presence.

We may feel nothing when we pray or minister to another, but the absence of the *sense* of God's presence is sometimes only in our subjective feelings, not in what is objectively taking place.

PART THREE

How To Pray

7

The Model Prayer

This, then, is how you should pray. (Matt. 6:9)

One day Jesus was praying in a certain place. His disciples must have been aware that he was praying because when he finished they said to him, 'Lord, teach *us* to pray, just as John taught his disciples' (emphasis mine, Luke 11:1). Jesus then said to them, 'When you pray, say: "Father, hallowed be your name, your kingdom come."' This became known as 'the Lord's Prayer'. Virtually the same prayer is repeated in the Sermon on the Mount (Matt. 6:9–13).

I want to write a separate book on the Lord's Prayer one day, but I felt I must give an outline of this magnificent prayer in this one. The Lord's Prayer provides an introduction on how to pray – it is the perfect prayer. It shows not only what we should say when we approach

71

God, but the pattern we should follow.

In the Sermon on the Mount, the Lord's Prayer emerged not in answer to the disciples' request but in the context of Jesus' teaching how *not* to pray. He had been telling the disciples not to pray like the hypocrites who love to pray 'standing in the synagogues and on the street corners to be seen by men' (Matt. 6:5). Jesus said of the ancient Pharisees, 'Everything they do is done for men to see' (Matt. 23:5).

We deduce from this that Rule Number One in how not to pray is praying to be seen by people. If your motive to pray is to make sure others see you pray or know that you do a bit of praying, your approach to prayer is quite wrong. It violates one of the most consistent principles of Jesus' teaching. He says the same thing about giving and fasting; if things like this are done to be 'seen' by people, then you do get your reward, yes – but that reward is merely *that people know* you prayed, gave or fasted. In a word: a pretty shabby reward (if you ask me) compared to what would have come from God alone had one done it entirely for his glory (John 5:44).

The Lord's Prayer is a prayer to be prayed – whether individually or together. An early Christian document called *The Didache* (known as 'the teaching of the twelve disciples') prescribed that Christians should repeat this prayer three times daily. I don't particularly recommend doing it that often, but it is a prayer that is commanded – it is put in the imperative mood: how you *must* pray. It is a corporate prayer. We pray, '*Our* Father'. Not only that, the command is how 'you' (second person plural) should pray. I might add that it is a correct prayer; we are told exactly what to say. This is a prayer approved of by God; praying this prayer is at least one time you can be sure that you pray in the will of God. Moreover, it is a complete prayer. It contains six petitions that include everything we may rightly wish from God.

This is not the only way to pray, neither is it only to be prayed in public – as some might suppose. It is a *pattern* prayer – the model prayer. Let the Lord's Prayer be your model, follow its petitions, its order; you can never outdo praying along these lines – whether in private or in public.

'Our Father . . .'

The prayer we normally pray should be addressed to God the Father. There is nothing wrong with addressing a prayer to Jesus (Luke 23:42; Acts 7:59), or to the Holy Spirit (otherwise, a lot of our hymnody got it wrong, as in 'Come, Holy Ghost, all-quickening fire'). But our praying, speaking generally, should recognise God the Creator and Redeemer as Father. Jesus said, 'This, then, is how you should pray: "Our Father . . ." ' (Matt. 6:9).

Some have objected to praying the Lord's Prayer because it does not end in Jesus' name. My reply: the moment we address God as *Father* we pray in Jesus' name. This is because we have no right to call God Father except that we have been brought to him through his Son, Jesus Christ.

Be careful about popular talk – 'Fatherhood of God'. It is absolutely true that the Fatherhood of God is essential Christian teaching, but there are those who take a 'universalist' perspective that is alien to Scripture. They would say that God is Father to everybody, whether or not they come to him through Jesus. Wrong. God is Father *only* through Jesus; hence the Lord's Prayer is to be prayed because it *assumes* Jesus is God's only Son and our Saviour. Furthermore, Jesus gave this prayer to the Church, not the world.

It also means that God is *personal*. The late Paul Tillich, a universalist, would call God 'the ground of all being'. This is very like pantheism ('everything is God'), although some prefer to call it panentheism – 'everything, all creation, is in God'. In any case, it makes God impersonal. In ancient times even the Jews would not address God as Father, but rather Sovereign Lord, King of the universe or, simply, *Adonai* – 'Lord'. But you and I are invited to call him *Father*, because that is what he is and who he is to those who come to God through Jesus.

Jesus equally points us to the *perfect* Father when he tells us to pray 'Our Father'. There are those who have great difficulty in calling God 'Father' because their only frame of reference for a father is a silent, absent, abusive, sulking, impossible-to-please or non-caring father. There are those, including older Christians, who can only call him 'Lord', 'God' or 'Lord God' – never 'Father' – all because of horrible connotations with the word 'father'. One should sympathise with this problem, one that is common to quite a few Christians. But we should remember that Jesus said, 'Anyone who has seen *me* has seen the Father' (emphasis mine, John 14:9). We must *think Jesus* when we call God our Father. He is the perfect father.

Not only that; our heavenly Father is always *present*. Human fathers will be absent. They cannot always be there. They can be busy, or preoccupied. They may put other things first. Some people grow up with an absentee father. Our Father is in heaven, yes; but is equally here – closer than our hands or our feet; closer than the air we breathe. He is but a cry away.

Jesus always prayed to his Father, and referred to him as 'Father'. The only time he addressed him as 'God' was when he cried out on the cross, 'My God, my God, why have you forsaken me?' (Matt. 27:46). That was the moment all our sins were transferred to Jesus (2 Cor. 5:21) and God turned his back on his one and only Son. A sense of fellowship between the Father and the Son was momentarily forfeited when Jesus bore our sins. It was the worst part of his suffering.

We therefore approach a Father whose justice was totally satisfied – once for all – by the shed blood of his Son. Remember that *expiation* is what the blood does for *us* (it atones for our sin); *propitiation* is what the blood does for God the Father. Therefore we approach a Father who accepts us as we are through his Son. This is why Jesus told us to pray 'Our Father', because his mission into the world was to die on a cross. He set the pattern for the praying that his people would do. The personal, perfect and ever-present Father calls us to pray, giving us the perfect prayer that leaves out nothing that we need.

'In heaven . . .'

Why does Jesus add these words, 'in heaven'? In a word: it puts us in our place. I connect this phrase 'in heaven' to these words: 'Do not be quick with your mouth, do not be hasty in your heart to utter anything before God. *God is in heaven and you are on earth*, so let your words be few' (emphasis mine, Eccles. 5:2–3). Psalm 115:3 also comes to mind: 'Our God is in heaven; he does whatever pleases him.' These words 'in heaven' remind us of how big and how great God is. It is a word also given partly to ensure that we never become overly familiar with him.

We have two things going on simultaneously here. First, as our *Father* we are reminded of his love and the intimacy he wants us to enjoy. Just as Jesus could refer to the Father as *abba* – an Aramaic word that means 'daddy' – so can we. And this cannot be stressed too much. We have been adopted into the family and are joint-heirs with Jesus

(Rom. 8:15; Eph. 1:5); as Jesus could call the Father 'daddy', so can we – and so we must! The Father loves us as much as he loves Jesus – we are co-heirs.

But at the same time the Father is *in heaven*. This means he is invisible – out of sight. You cannot see him; faith is required. When you can see the person you are talking with, you don't need to exercise faith that he or she is before your eyes. So although God is personal, he is also Spirit (John 4:24). He cannot be seen.

His being in heaven also means he is independent. When one is as high as the heavens are above the earth, you know you can't snap your finger at the person, expecting immediate service. You are in your place. You, instead, are on the begging end – waiting for him to grant us mercy. According to the writer to the Hebrews, the first thing we ask for when we pray is *mercy* (Heb. 4:16). Or as it is put in one of the psalms of ascents, 'As the eyes of slaves look to the hand of their master, as the eyes of a maid look to the hand of her mistress, so our eyes look to the LORD our God, till he shows us his mercy' (Ps. 123:2–3). Never forget that the God of the Bible continues to say, 'I will have mercy on whom I will have mercy' (Exod. 33:19; Rom. 9:15). Never forget too that God can give or withhold mercy and be equally just either way.

His independence also means that he will not be controlled by us. He is not tied to us. He is not dependent on us. He does not need our wisdom. He is not looking to us in order to know what to do next. The future is as clear to him as the past. He does not consult a higher authority for wisdom, he does not look to the highest archangel whom he made – much less does he appeal to finite people like you and me. Because there is no greater, he decides by himself (Heb. 6:13). Therefore when we acknowledge that God is *in heaven* we affirm his independence from his creation and our dependence on him.

There is more: God is inscrutable. This means it is impossible fully to understand him. You can never figure him out. You may think you know him so very well, then realise that you don't. You think you understand him, then you realise you don't. He is in heaven. You cannot predict what he will do. Never say that you know for sure what God is going to do; he is in heaven and you are on earth. He is in control and you and I are not. 'Oh, the depth of the riches of the wisdom and knowledge of God! How unsearchable his judgments, and his paths beyond tracing out! Who has known the mind of the Lord? Or who has been his counsellor?' (Rom. 11:33–34)

The phrase 'in heaven' is also language of accommodation. God has been accommodating us with language from the beginning of time. For example, when he said, 'I will go down and see if what they have done is as bad as the outcry that has reached me' (Gen. 9:21), he already knew the truth – totally – but spoke on Abraham's level. The same is true when he said to Abraham, 'Now I know you fear God' (Gen. 22:12), but Abraham's obedience did not take God by surprise. God speaks to us where we are. So when he says that he is in 'heaven', God isn't limited to space or to a place. Solomon put it best: 'Will God really dwell on earth? The heavens, even the highest heaven, cannot contain you' (1 Kgs. 8:27).

'Hallowed be your name . . .'

This is actually the first petition of our model prayer, but keep in mind that the Lord's Prayer is a *pattern* prayer. It is not only to be prayed word for word from time to time; the *order* is of great importance. The words 'Our Father in heaven', followed by the first petition 'hallowed be your name', are designed partly to keep us from rushing into God's presence and clicking our fingers – expecting him to jump. We are not allowed to do that. Therefore not only is the content inspired but also the order; the sequence of each petition has a purpose. Here God is teaching us, 'Do not rush into my presence with your requests; recognise who I am before you do that.'

In other words, the Lord's Prayer makes us *pause to worship*. Proper praying is done when we take time to worship God before we come out with our prayer lists. It is not unlike Paul's words, 'Do not be anxious about anything, but in everything, by prayer and petition, *with thanksgiving*, present your requests to God' (Phil. 4:6). Thanksgiving is an essential part of worship, and so it is here. This petition of the Lord's Prayer is inserted that we will worship – and that God will be given his rightful place in our hearts by our affirming *his* interests before we come to ours. 'Hallowed be your name.'

By the way, have you been guilty of rushing into God's presence – without any true regard for the One whom you are addressing?

And yet we've all done this. It is an easy thing to do. But God does not say, 'STOP – don't talk to me any more until you take time to worship me for a moment or two.' No, he does not do that. He is always a very present help in times of trouble (Ps. 46:1). There are often times when we cry out to him without thinking to say, 'hallowed be your name'. There are times when we can only think to cry out 'GOD!' The same God who accommodates us with language also understands when we turn to him in desperation and do not pause to worship. When he was desperate, King David prayed, 'O LORD, turn Ahithophel's counsel into foolishness' (2 Sam. 15:31).

However, the pattern that is set out in the Lord's Prayer is the ideal way to pray. It should be generally followed. We are reminded that there is an architectural blueprint God has already designed for us if we want to be devoted people of prayer.

Jesus thus requires us to acknowledge the Father's name. It is as though Jesus says to us, 'Don't move on in praying until you acknowledge my Father's name.' Jesus was demonstrating a jealous loyalty to his Father. After all, all that Jesus ever did was with the Father's name in mind.

'The Son can do nothing by himself; he can only do what he sees his Father doing, because whatever the Father does the Son also does' (John 5:19). 'I have come in my Father's name' (John 5:43). Everything Jesus did – his words and his acts – was to uphold the name of the Father.

The first petition, then, is a petition of praise and worship – 'hallowed be your name'. Note: it is not 'holy is your name'; God's name is holy anyway. It is a petition, 'hallowed *be* your name' – a prayer that the Father's name will be *treated as holy*.

There are two essential things in a name. The first is identity. In ancient times a person's name was revelatory – in other words, it was closely related to one's calling. Abraham meant 'of a great multitude'. Sarah meant 'princess'. God's name was *Yahweh*: 'I AM WHO I AM', 'I will be who I will be' (Exod. 3:14). In the Lord's Prayer we pray that the Father will be universally recognised for who he truly is.

The second essential thing in a name is reputation: 'A good name is more desirable than great riches' (Prov. 22:1). Moses appealed to God's name and reputation when he interceded for Israel (Num. 14:13–16). Joshua did exactly the same thing (Josh. 7:9). As Jesus was jealous for his Father's name, so should you and I be.

What Jesus wants you and me to pray is that *all* will respect his Father's name. Everything we do must bring honour and glory to his name. We should want the whole world to revere the Father's name. It is the first petition we put to him: that we – and everybody else on the planet – will participate in the awesomeness of the Father's name.

You may not have realised it, but when you pray the Lord's Prayer you pledge to be accountable to that name. You cannot pray, 'hallowed be your name' and then live in a manner that is contrary to his honour. You cannot pray that all will recognise the awesomeness of that name when you do not mirror this plea yourself by a life that shows reverence for that name. You do not want people to misuse or abuse that name, neither will you ever drag God's name into your life in a way that does not reflect his holiness.

To pray 'hallowed be your name', then, is a pledge to treat his name as holy as you represent him to the world. You are the nearest that some will ever come to seeing the Father's face.

This petition is even a prayer for the advancement of his name. It is a prayer that the name of the Father will be held in the honour that it deserves, that people will never think of him without highest reverence. It is a prayer that the whole world will bow before God. It is therefore a prayer that God's name will be treated as holy, that God himself will move on men and women everywhere to hallow his name; for it is a prayer that God will manifest his glory. God's name and glory are inseparable (Isa. 42:8).

I pray you will never forget the gravity of the very first petition of the Lord's Prayer.

'Your kingdom come . . .'

This is the second petition, and Jesus now turns our attention to what interests God. I fear that most of us care about what interests *us* – our needs, our wants, our selfish desires. We live in the me-generation: 'what's in it for me?' We never seem to ask, 'what's in it for God?' So much praying is man-centred and a form of manipulation – to seek God for what we ourselves want in this world.

Jesus makes us focus on God and his interests. I myself was deeply gripped many years ago by some of the sermons of Jonathan Edwards. He showed things about God I had not thought of. For example, what Satan cannot successfully counterfeit in us is a love for God's interest in the world – God's glory. Satan cannot produce a love for the glory of God. When you truly focus on what interests God, you cross over into the supernatural. Crossing over into the supernatural defies a natural explanation. The most natural kind of praying is to focus on our own needs and wishes. The Lord's Prayer enables us to cross over into the supernatural when we focus *from our hearts* on what interests God.

And how is focusing on God's interest done? You begin to do this when you pray 'your kingdom come'. The highest honour and privilege on this earth is to be consciously in God's kingdom. 'I am your king,' God said to ancient Israel who wanted to be like other nations and have their own king (1 Sam. 8:7; Isa. 43:15).

The phrase 'kingdom of God' (kingdom of heaven) is used in more than one way, however, in the New Testament. In the Sermon on the Mount it mainly refers to the internal reign and rule of the Holy Spirit in our hearts. Whether you take its meaning in the Sermon on the Mount or in Luke's account of the Lord's Prayer (Luke 11:2), the kingdom refers primarily to the inner testimony of the Spirit – not an outward, visible kingdom. The kingdom of heaven refers to God's sovereign and gracious occupation in the *hearts* of his people.

Having said so much about the kingdom, Jesus therefore counsels us to pray 'your kingdom come'. We are to pray that the kingdom would be our living experience and possession. That is what interests God and that is what should interest us. All of the theological principles Jesus taught about the kingdom of heaven are assumed in this petition, 'your kingdom come'.

The new birth, being 'born again', is the prerequisite to seeing the kingdom (John 3:3). But presumably anybody praying the Lord's Prayer has already been born again since this prayer was given to Jesus' own disciples. However, I would simply say that if a person who is not born again prays this prayer, then he or she is *praying* to be born again.

But when the Christian prays for the coming of the kingdom, it means an utter submission to the total rule of God over that person. It may mean suffering. After all, we enter the kingdom of God through hardship and suffering (Acts 14:22).

One could also argue that praying for the kingdom to come is a plea for the kind of miracles that accompanied Jesus' ministry. I myself pray for this every day. But we must pray for this with the view to it being in God's interest, not our own. The heart is so deceitful (Jer. 17:9) and we *could* conceivably pray for signs and wonders with a selfish motive.

And yet the petition 'your kingdom come' could even be a plea for the Second Coming of Jesus. There is nothing wrong, and everything right, about praying for the kingdom with this in mind. John prayed, 'Come, Lord Jesus' (Rev. 22:20). Furthermore, Paul spoke of the kingdom in this way, referring to Jesus as the judge of the living and the dead in view of 'his appearing and his kingdom' (2 Tim. 4:1).

The kingdom is God's special interest, and the Lord's Prayer is in a sense a teaching tool to help us focus on what means so much to God. Nothing is more important to him than the kingdom, and that is why it is the second petition in our model prayer.

'Your will be done . . .'

Petition number three is an elaboration of the previous plea, 'your kingdom come'. The kingdom of God is in itself the quintessence of God's will, but to pray 'your will be done' means not only to want the kingdom, but to accept whatever God's will is. When you pray 'your will be done', it means that you accept it, you approve of it, you honour it. You may not always know what God's will is. Whereas Jesus' prayer in Gethsemane, 'May your will be done', was prayed knowing precisely what he had to do (Matt. 26:42), many of us pray these words because we *don't* know what God's will is. But we accept it, whatever it is. Sometimes it is like signing a blank cheque and letting God fill it out. This is *partly* what Jesus means by this third petition, 'your will be done'.

But there is more to it than that. When we pray 'your will be done', we acknowledge that *God has a will*. We don't give him input and help him to see what he ought to want to do. He already has a will of his own. Therefore when I pray 'your will be done', in that moment I acknowledge that he has already decided what he has willed to do. We don't advise him on what we think it should be.

By God's 'will' it means that God is independent from us; he has a will of his own. It means that he thinks for himself; he has a mind of his own. In a word: God has a plan. I refer again to that architectural blueprint that he has drawn up from the foundation of the world.

And yet God's will is also understood as his Word (Holy Scripture) – which is his revealed will. The Word of God is the revealed will of God. If you want to know God's will, get to know his Word. The Bible contains all we need for knowing God, how to live a life that is pleasing to him. Therefore when we pray 'your will be done', we pledge to live according to his Word – what he has already revealed. The same God who gave us his Word is not going to lead you in a direction contrary to it.

Another aspect of God's will is called his secret will. This is what he has decided about you and me, including the details of our lives. ' "For I know the plans I have for you," declares the LORD, "plans to prosper you and not to harm you, plans to give you hope and a future" ' (Jer. 29:11). God has a plan of his own for our career, future, anointing, gifts, job, whether to marry or whom to marry – indeed, every detail we might be curious about. 'He chose our inheritance for us' (Ps. 47:4). When we pray 'your will be done', it is accepting whatever God has in mind for us. As I said, you approve of it; you honour it because you want what God wants. You may not know what it is, but if it is what he wants, that is good enough.

But this petition is equally an appeal to God for his will to be carried out. We are therefore appealing to him to carry out his will, to bring it to pass, each time we pray the Lord's Prayer. It is much the same as praying 'hallowed be your name'; we want the world to reverence the God of the Bible. So too we appeal to God that his will, known to him from the foundation of the world, will be openly manifest in the world.

In other words, we pray for the accomplishment of God's will. When Jesus adds these words, 'on earth as it is in heaven', it is an acknowledgement that God's will is *being done perfectly in heaven.* In heaven there is no sin, no rebellion, no unbelief. There will be no more revolt in heaven, as happened long before the Fall of humankind (2 Pet. 2:4; Jude 6). All the inhabitants worship God without any constraint or reluctance.

Our prayer, then, is that God's will in heaven shall be mirrored on earth – without any interference in between, without any reluctance or rebellion.

Question: should we pray for what will possibly never be accomplished until the end of the age? I answer: yes. I think of poverty, for example. I think of injustices in this world. There are things that we long to see happen that have not happened. I will pray on and on and on. That is partly what this petition means. But what we *can* fully expect and hope for now, if it is left up to us, is that there will be no revolt left in *us*, no rebellion in *us*, no stubbornness towards God's will in *us*, no reluctance in *us*. But at the same time we do all we can to carry out God's will when we see injustice before our very eyes. I can't answer for you, the world or the church, but I can answer for myself. I will do all I can.

Some say that since there is no sickness, poverty or injustice in heaven, it is God's will that there be no sickness, poverty or injustice on earth. Some take the third petition to mean that everybody should be healed and nobody should have financial problems. The problem is, taking this line smacks of forcing God to do in the here and now what we think he should do. Do not forget that God has a secret will; there are things known only to him.

Accepting God's will includes dignifying him if all of our requests are not granted. Don't delude yourself that you can force God into a mould and tell him what he has to do. That is not what the third petition intends to convey. The purpose of this petition, 'your will be done on earth as it is in heaven', is to help us to bow to his will, whatever it may be, and let him be God.

'Give us today our daily bread . . .'

This fourth petition changes from 'your' to 'our'. It is the first reference to us. And yet the first three petitions are *for* us! What the late Cardinal Basil Hume said a few days before he died is absolutely true, 'What God wants is always what is best for us.'

But in this petition we are given the green light to focus on ourselves. And yet God still sets the agenda – he knows our true need.

The petition 'give us today our daily bread' relates to what God will supply anyway, for he has already promised this (Matt. 6:25ff; Phil. 4:19). So there is nothing new about this in our model prayer. And yet – imagine this – the great Creator and Sovereign God of heaven and earth stoops to where we are. 'For this is what the high and lofty One says – he who lives for ever, whose name is holy: "I live in a high and holy place, but also with him who is contrite and lowly in spirit, to revive the spirit of the lowly and to revive the heart of the contrite" ' (Isa. 57:15). As someone put it so well, 'Don't worry about praying over small things; with God everything is small.'

And yet does it surprise you that the first petition that focuses on us has to do with our food? We may have thought that God would bring in the spiritual petitions first! But no. The first petition we ask for ourselves is for our daily bread. He regards this as what we are to pray for first. He begins with the body. God chose to give us bodies, and he deals with this first.

I reckon the reason for the order is partly because it is extremely difficult to cope spiritually when we are hungry, thirsty, tired, or deep in debt. William Booth, founder of the Salvation Army, said it is hard to preach the gospel to someone with an empty stomach. Likewise, it is hard to pray when we are overwhelmed with daily emotional, material and physical problems. This petition is a reminder that God knows our situation and what we are like; that we have to eat to live. Therefore God made this petition a priority over the spiritual need.

'Daily bread' does not only mean food in the literal sense, however. It is a phrase that covers all our *essential needs*. 'Bread' in Hebrew means all kinds of nutriment. But more than that, it refers to everything non-spiritual that is essential to life: physical needs, emotional needs, material needs, financial needs. This petition covers everything that God knows to be essential for us.

Jesus originally addressed an agrarian society. In those

days, one crop failure spelled disaster. Not only that — labourers were paid daily for the work they did. The pay was so low that it was almost impossible to save any money. One day's pay purchased the food for that day alone. This petition, then, was no empty rhetoric. People in those days lived from day to day, unlike most of us in the Western world today.

This petition therefore refers to food, shelter, clothing, having a job, income — even sleep. Try praying effectively without sleep! This petition includes all that is essential — the ability to work, having strength, intelligence, peace.

There is a further purpose in this petition: to warn against greed and to teach us gratitude. This petition does not hint at comforts and luxuries — only what is essential. As for gratitude, God loves gratitude; he hates ingratitude. This petition should make us thankful for the way God supplies our daily needs. It should make us realise our debt to God every single day.

We are all utterly dependent upon God for these essential things. We must never — ever — take for granted the essentials that God provides us with.

> *'Forgive us our debts, as we also have forgiven our debtors . . .'*

Having dealt with the non-spiritual essentials of life, Jesus now turns to our spiritual needs. I suppose this petition has made liars out of more people than any document in history. I say this because it is a *plea* and a *promise*. The plea is for forgiveness of our own sins; the promise is a statement that we also *have* forgiven those who have sinned against us. I fear that untold millions have prayed this petition and either didn't know what they were saying, didn't want to know, or didn't mean it.

In Luke's rendition we are to say, 'Forgive us our sins, for we also *forgive* everyone who sins against us' (emphasis mine, Luke 11:4). Note that the promise we make to God is in the present tense; we *forgive* everyone who sins against us. In Matthew's account we declare that we *have forgiven* our debtors. In other words, we claim that we have already done it. Have you?

Do you realise what you are saying when you utter this fifth petition of the Lord's Prayer? First, we pray for the forgiveness of our own sins. The Greek word 'debt' means *what is owed*. It is a word used interchangeably with sins (see also Matt. 6:14f). What we owe to God is pure obedience; the debt is that we have come short of what we owed – hence, our sin. Second, we pray that we will be let off the hook. The word 'forgive' means to 'let be' or 'send away', and it is a prayer that God will overlook our debts. Instead of having to pay the debt, we ask that God will wipe it away. Third, we pledge to God that we have already done this with others. We dare not ask God to do what we ourselves would not do. So this petition has a promise attached to it – namely, our word of honour that we have let others off the hook.

This is not a prayer for salvation or justification. It is not a 'sinner's prayer', like saying, 'God, have mercy on me, a sinner' (see Luke 18:13). The proof that this fifth petition is not a prayer for salvation is (1) the underlying assumption in the prayer from the beginning is that we are already in the family of God, and (2) we are saved by faith alone apart from works (Eph. 2:8–9). If we were justified or saved on the basis of having forgiven others, it would be salvation by works. After all, I doubt there is a greater 'good work' under the sun than letting your enemy off the hook.

The Lord's Prayer is a believer's prayer; only a truly converted person can pray this prayer from the heart. It shows too that saved people need the daily forgiveness of their sins as much as we need daily bread. If we say we have no sin, we deceive ourselves and the truth is not in us (1 John 1:8).

What, then, is the purpose of this petition? First, to keep us in unbroken and conscious fellowship with the Father. If we are to have fellowship with the Father, we must walk in the light. If we claim to have fellowship with him and yet walk in darkness (e.g. not totally forgiving those who have hurt us), we walk in darkness; 'we lie and do not live by the truth' (1 John 1:6–7).

Second, to help keep us from being self-righteous. This is something that all of us, if we are transparently honest, must fight all the time. I know I do. I wish I could write a book entitled *How to Overcome Self-righteousness*, but that would be like writing a book called *Humility and How I Obtained It*! When Jesus clearly gives us a petition to pray that includes 'forgive us our sins', it should be enough to keep us from claiming to be without sin. It is self-righteous to say, 'I am beyond the need to pray this prayer because I don't sin.' This petition, if we take it seriously, will help us realise how sinful our self-righteousness is before God. Had Jesus envisaged that his followers could reach a state of sinlessness at some stage, he would not have given a prayer for the Church that included asking for the forgiveness of our sins. Jesus gave us this *because* sinlessness is not possible in this life (1 John 1:8). Sinlessness is reserved for glorification (Rom. 8:30), when we shall be like Jesus (1 John 3:2).

Third, inheriting the kingdom is seriously jeopardised when we don't forgive others as we have been forgiven. How would *you* feel if the forgiveness of all your sins were granted *in proportion* to the manner in which you have forgiven others? That is precisely what Jesus means in this petition. Furthermore, if you want to know how important this petition is, consider that it is the only one of the six that Jesus elaborates on at the conclusion of this prayer. When the prayer is finished, the next thing he says is: '*For* if you forgive men when they sin against you, your heavenly Father will also forgive you. But if you do not forgive men their sins, your Father will not forgive your sins' (emphasis mine, Matt. 6:14–15).

The assumption in this petition is that we need to be forgiven. I repeat: Jesus takes for granted that we will sin and need to be forgiven. However, he is not talking about sinning deliberately and consciously – such as breaking the Ten Commandments. He is talking about the failure to please God in all our thoughts, words and deeds – sixty seconds a minute, sixty minutes an hour, twenty-four hours a day, seven days a week, fifty-two weeks a year. We all fall short and need forgiveness.

Jesus also assumes that people have hurt us. Not only have we come short of God's glory, but others have too – and have offended us in one way or another. We all have a story to tell – some have suffered more than others. Some have been betrayed, raped, abused, lied about, abandoned – the list is endless.

So Jesus assumes that: (1) we will need to be forgiven of all we have done, and (2) there will be those we must forgive (no matter what they have done to hurt us). In my book *Total Forgiveness* I elaborate on how you know you have forgiven others totally – it means you don't repeat what they did, or let them feel afraid of you or guilty; in other words, you let them save face, you protect them from their darkest secret and you keep on forgiving – as long as you live. (Obviously if the 'darkest secret' involves something that is actually *illegal*, this is a different matter.) You forgive to enjoy the rule and reign of the Holy Spirit – which is inheriting the kingdom of heaven. By the way, the greater the suffering (or hurt you feel), the greater the comfort, blessing or, in some cases, anointing that is promised to you (if you dignify the trial and totally forgive the person/persons).

'And lead us not into temptation, but deliver us from the evil one . . .'

We come now to the sixth and final petition. Some say there are seven, considering that this petition is in two parts.

In the hymn that provides part of the title for this book, ''Ere you left your room this morning, did you think to pray?' there is also a verse: 'When you met with great temptation, did you think to pray?' Jesus asks us to pray 'lead us not into temptation'.

However, this is a very difficult petition to understand. Someone could infer from this petition that if temptation comes your way, it is because God led you into it. This way, you can blame God if you are tempted, say some.

This theological difficulty turns on the translation of *peirasmon* – the Greek word that means either 'temptation', 'testing', or 'trial'. I conclude that Jesus basically means that we pray, 'lead us not into a time of testing, or trial'. The reason I say this is because James says, 'When tempted, no one should say, "God is tempting me." For God cannot be tempted by evil, nor does he tempt anyone; but each one is tempted when, by his own evil desire, he is dragged away and enticed' (James 1:13–14). Therefore I conclude that 'temptation' is not the best translation; instead, it is 'trial' or 'testing'.

But that does not solve the dilemma. James also said that we should count it 'pure joy' when we fall into various kinds of troubles or trials (James 1:2). If we are to count testing as pure joy, then why pray to avoid that which is designed to bring pure joy? I believe the answer is: we should not enter into the day *looking* for a trial, or testing. That would not be a healthy way to lead your life. Put another way, I am not to begin the day by saying, 'Oh good, I pray a severe trial today because this *will* bring me great joy.' That would be silly. In fact, Jesus counsels us to pray that we are certainly *not* allowed to enter a time of trial or testing.

On the other hand, if God does allow a time of testing after we have prayed not to have it, you may be sure that God has a purpose in mind in letting it happen. The Greek *perepisite* in James 1:2 really means when you 'fall' into a time of testing. That means it *happened* to you; you did not go looking for it. But if you pray that you will not be allowed to face trial or testing, but still 'fall' into it, it is then you may consider it pure joy. In a word: our prayer to God is that we will be spared unnecessary suffering.

We know we will be tested one way or another nearly every day. I think Jesus is referring to a severe kind of trial; it is right to pray that such will not be your lot.

But what if God allows circumstances in your life that means you are unexpectedly faced with temptation – as in sexual temptation? Joseph was – when Potiphar's wife flirted with him day after day and tried to get him to go to bed with her (Gen. 39:7). Joseph was tempted, but he refused. It was a very important test for Joseph, and I think God allowed this in order that Joseph could see for himself that he had passed a major test. After all, it is only a matter of time before most of us will be faced with sexual temptation. We must overcome in this area if we expect to be greatly used of God for very long. Billy Graham said some time ago that it seems Satan gets 75 per cent of the best of God's servants who fall through them giving in to sexual temptation. Nothing brings disgrace on the name of God and the Church like sexual scandal. But Jesus said to pray in any case that you are not led into such a testing.

The best way to avoid sexual sin is to avoid the temptation. Most of us have a pretty shrewd idea what and who is likely to tempt us – and where this might take place. *Don't go there*. 'Do not think about how to gratify the desires of the sinful nature' (Rom. 13:14).

But Jesus added, 'but deliver us from the evil one'. He says this partly because testing could be orchestrated by the devil. Satan certainly will move in quickly once he sees an opportunity. What could have begun in the flesh could become the very thing that Satan exploits, causing the temptation to double or treble in its intensity. For as soon as Satan sees we are being tempted, he will exploit it to the hilt. This is partly why Jesus says, 'but deliver us from the evil one'.

In the same way, once a time of testing comes, be sure that Satan will move in. He will put thoughts into our minds, such as: 'God is not pleased with you or you would not be in this circumstance'; 'curse God now that he has let this happen to you'; 'this shows you are not a Christian'; 'resisting temptation isn't worth it – give in to it'; 'it is folly to dignify this trial – God has forsaken you and let you down'; 'if there were a God and he loves you, you wouldn't be in this mess'. Remember that the devil's job description is to accuse – it is what he does (Rev. 12:11).

What are we to do? We are to dignify the trial. That means to bless God, not curse him. We say something like this: 'Lord, I know you love me and have permitted this for a purpose. I want to pass this test with flying colours. I worship and adore you – I will not give in.' It also means not to grumble (God does not like that – see 1 Corinthians 10:10, where Paul refers to their grumbling). It also means to let every trial have its full purpose. In other words, don't try to get a trial over with quickly. After all, it will end. Every trial has its own built-in time scale. When it is over, be thankful, but aim for the joy of knowing you dignified it to the maximum degree.

The classic rendition of the Lord's Prayer (AV) is 'deliver us from evil'. But the majority of scholars believe that the Greek word *ponerou* with the definite article really means 'the evil one', a reference to Satan. It is a prayer that we will not get caught in the devil's snare, but be spared of any success on his part. What is more, dignifying the trial is the best way to be delivered from the evil one. If we don't accuse God ('why me?') or if we don't complain the whole time, but rejoice in all circumstances, *Satan will utterly fail with us*.

Keep in mind too that the devil will take full advantage of any bitterness in us. This is why total forgiveness is essential if we are to be delivered from his power. Satan exploits bitterness and grudges. Paul said, 'I have forgiven in the sight of Christ . . . in order that Satan might not outwit us. For we are not unaware of his schemes' (2 Cor. 2:10–11). As the New Living Bible puts it, 'A further reason for forgiveness is to keep from being out-smarted by Satan.'

Remember the 'three Rs' of spiritual warfare: recognise, refuse, resist. Recognise the devil – that is, when an evil thought comes, a thought that God would not have put there, see it at once as the devil. Refuse. That means do not entertain the thought. Refuse to give the evil thought any attention whatever. Resist. If the devil keeps coming back, resist him! We have the promise, 'Resist the devil, and he will flee from you' (James 4:7).

The devil knows his end; he knows that his time is short (Matt. 8:29; Rev. 12:10–12). The next time the devil reminds you of his past, remind him of his future (Rev. 20:10)!

The beautiful phrase 'for yours is the kingdom and the

power and the glory for ever. Amen' may not have been a part of the original manuscript. But there is nothing wrong in ending the prayer with it! In my day at Westminster Chapel we prayed it every single Sunday morning for twenty-five years, ending with the sublime words, 'For thine is the kingdom, and the power, and the glory for ever and ever. Amen.'

Like it or not, we do not outgrow one single petition in the Lord's Prayer. We will need to pray these petitions – or at least follow the pattern of it – every day until Jesus comes. There is no perfection here below (1 John 1:8). It is a prayer we pray again and again and again. What is more, you will love this prayer more and more and more. Finally, it will help you to learn how to pray more than any other aid or example given in the Bible.

One of the points I have wanted to make in this chapter is not only the meaning of the items Jesus wants us to pray daily, but also that we must not rush into God's presence as if to demand that he do this or that. The Lord's Prayer is the ideal prayer and is the pattern that Jesus sets for us to follow. But do not be governed by a legalistic approach. The Spirit, not the letter, must guide us. The main thing we learn from the Lord's Prayer, I think, is that we are primarily to seek God's face, not his hand.

In other words, it is fellowship with the Father that Jesus wants for us. Seeking his face means desiring to know him intimately and wanting the sense of his smile. Seeking his hand is mainly asking him to do things for us. We are to seek both, but do our best to follow the order Jesus gives.

Applying the Lord's Prayer

In your private quiet time. I believe that the greatest fringe benefit of being a Christian is the privilege of prayer – it doesn't get better than that. But every new Christian needs to learn how to pray. If you want to get it right, follow the Lord's Prayer.

The moment we recognise that our Father is in heaven we are put in our place. No snapping of the finger for him to stand at attention is allowed. It is unthinkable. We go to him on bended knee. You never outgrow that.

There are three verses that have largely governed me, all of which I will deal with later: Hebrews 4:16, 1 John 4:16 and Philippians 4:6. It may help you to remember that two of them are 4:16:

Let us then approach the throne of grace with confidence, so that we may receive mercy and find grace to help us in our time of need. (Heb. 4:16)

And so we know and rely on the love God has for us. (1 John 4:16)

Philippians 4:6 reminds us to bring our petitions to God *with thanksgiving*. All three of these verses keep us from approaching God in a rushed, selfish, cavalier manner. When we ask for mercy, we realise we have no bargaining power. When we pause to affirm the love God has for us, we equally find ourselves dependent on him. We show gratitude at the same time as we ask for things. God wants us to know *him*.

I'm sorry to sound critical, but I sometimes feel as if I could die a thousand deaths when I hear certain preachers today. They often give the distinct impression that prayer is all about getting what you want. This is a far cry from the New Testament. We worship first, then present our petitions. We bring before him our physical needs, followed by the spiritual. And never underestimate the importance of total forgiveness.

The Lord's Prayer is designed to help us to know God – what he is like and how to experience him.

Praying in public. Have you prayed publicly before? You may well be asked to pray aloud in front of others. It is a scary thing to do the first time.

When I was a younger pastor I asked a man to pray publicly without warning him. He told me later he thought he was going to have a heart attack. When I saw the look on his face, I thought I was going to have a heart attack! And yet you may be asked to pray one day without being told in advance.

The Lord's Prayer is your model when praying publicly. Don't forget that it was given to the disciples, addressed to them in the second person plural. Therefore try to remember the general pattern and the contents.

Let me suggest an outline for a public prayer: *Heavenly Father, thank you for your goodness and mercy. Thank you for the privilege of prayer. Thank you for sending your Son to die on a cross for us. Hasten the day when all people see that Jesus is Lord to your glory. Have mercy on us as a nation. Bless our leaders and give them wisdom. Bless the government, the policemen, the firemen, the doctors and nurses, those in hospital. Have mercy on those who are in the military. Bless your people throughout the world. May your church grow this very day. Grant unity to the body of Christ. Forgive us our sins; we forgive those who have hurt us. May your providential care spare us from the wiles of the devil. Guide us by your Holy Spirit. In Jesus' name. Amen.*

This prayer generally follows the Lord's Prayer without repeating it. You can build on this. You will reach a place where you can soar in public praying, but try to begin each prayer with praise and thankfulness.

One of the difficulties with public praying is that you are often more conscious of being heard by those around you than you are by God himself. But you can eventually overcome this to some degree and reach a point where you can call on God with virtually no self-consciousness concerning other people listening.

Any public praying should be filled with worship and praise to God. Focusing on God, not our needs, honours him.

Each of us, has to crawl before we can walk. By praying the Lord's Prayer, we can crawl and walk at the same time. It is the best way to begin, and yet you never improve on it — even if you have been serving the Lord for dozens of years. We all pray prayers that are self-serving and not exactly in God's will. But when you pray the Lord's Prayer, or build on it, you may be sure you are getting it right when you pray.

8

Showing Gratitude

Do not be anxious about anything, but in
everything, by prayer and petition, with
thanksgiving, present your requests to God.

(Phil. 4:6)

It is not every day that God speaks to me through one of
my own sermons. I reckon I preached about 3,500
sermons in my twenty-five years in Westminster. (We have
something like 3,270 of them available on the internet.) No
doubt God spoke to me personally many times as I
preached, but I only remember one of those times for sure.
It was when we were in our series of sermons in Philippians
(1985–9). When we got to Philippians 4:6, as I unfolded the
text and came upon the words *with thanksgiving*, I was
shaken rigid. I could not wait to finish preaching so that I
could rush to the vestry, fall on my face, and repent for my

years of ingratitude. I can't remember exactly what I said as I preached or how I said it, but for some reason I was made to see *how little* I had actually thanked the Lord for things he had done.

I sat at my desk on that Sunday – 13 November 1988 – after I returned to the vestry. I made a promise to God – that I would be a thankful man for the rest of my life. I *so* wanted to make up for those years when I had taken God's goodness for granted. I made a further promise: that I would review every day for the rest of my life, one day at a time, and thank God for literally every single thing that was worth thanking him for.

God began to talk to me something like this; I am not meaning an audible voice or anything like that. But the impression on my soul was so deep that an audible voice would not have made me feel much worse. The impression came like this:

'R.T., I have been good to you.'

'Yes, Lord, I know this.'

'Are you thankful?'

'Yes, Lord, you know I'm thankful.'

'But you haven't told me.'

'Of course I have, Lord. You know I am thankful.'

'Do you remember how you were so fearful of not getting through Oxford University because you were intimidated by the system and the other students around you, in that they were so bright and had been brought up in the British educational system? You, knowing you were from Kentucky [where educational standards were not very high], were terrified you would never get through Oxford. I got you through it, didn't I?'

'Yes Lord.'

'But you never thanked me.'

'Lord, you *know* I'm thankful.'

'But you never *told* me.'

I felt horrible. That is not all. It seemed that the Lord began reminding me of dozens and dozens of good things he had done for me – allowing me to be the minister of Westminster Chapel, meeting certain people, having the best friends of my life, giving us such a beautiful place to live in London, writing books – the list seemed endless.

'Lord, you must know I have been thankful.'

'But you never told me.'

I keep a journal, so that is how I remember the date of this 'conversation' – 13 November 1988. On the Monday morning, 14 November 1988, I began a practice I have kept up every day since (it is now almost twenty years). As I review the events of the day before, I *thank the Lord for every single thing*. And guess what? It takes about thirty seconds! It doesn't take long! All God wants of us is to say 'thank you'. That's what he is waiting to hear from us.

You may say, as I did, 'But he knows I am thankful.' My reply is: TELL HIM.

On one occasion Jesus healed ten lepers, but only one of them came back to say thank you to Jesus. Instead of praising this leper for his gratitude, Jesus asked, 'Where are the other nine?' (Luke 17:17). God notices ingratitude.

On that day – 13 November 1988 – I felt so convicted of my ingratitude that my mind drifted to the words of the late Bob George, a deacon of Westminster Chapel. Mr George was fond of saying something that I repeated from the pulpit early in my ministry there. I had asked: 'How many of you out there in this congregation have never yet led a soul to Christ?' Mr George said it made him feel awful. 'Here I was, aged sixty, and I had never led a soul to Christ.' He vowed to make up for the wasted years. I felt the same way; I wanted to make up for the years of not thanking the Lord.

When we began our Pilot Light ministry in 1982

(witnessing on the streets to passers-by), who do you suppose was the first to join us? Yes, Mr George – carrying out his vow of making up for the years he had not witnessed to the lost. The last time I asked him about this, he had led over 500 people to pray the 'sinner's prayer'. Were they all saved? Probably not. But some of them were – and one of them eventually went into the Anglican ministry.

I felt the same way about being thankful. I have sought every day since to be a man of gratitude.

In this section on 'How to Pray' I am putting to you that gratitude must accompany your prayers. This is how to pray. Thank the Lord for everything you can think of – as soon as possible. It doesn't take long!

I will now share something a little bit personal with you. You of course must come up with your own time and manner of a quiet time. I do not want to impose what I do upon you. But if any of this helps, good!

I began my quiet time this morning (with a cup of coffee), as always, by welcoming the Holy Spirit. I always do this. 'Welcome, Holy Spirit' I say each morning. I then ask for the sprinkling of the blood of Jesus to be applied to my mind and heart by the Holy Spirit. I have my own little routine in this connection that I have followed for many years. The next thing I do is to turn to my journal. I go through every item I have written down, thanking the Lord for everything from the previous day, one by one. As it happens, today, as I write this, it is 25 January 2008, and this is what happened yesterday that I thanked the Lord for: (1) some impressions I put down in my journal – which I found edifying, (2) the particular prayer requests I felt good about (I almost always write down any fresh request), (3) a lovely breakfast with a bluegrass singer from my state of Kentucky (who phoned and welcomed me to our new town in Tennessee – he is a neighbour), (4) the CDs and the DVD he gave us – which Louise and I played and enjoyed, (5) the progress I made in writing this very book, (6) helping us shop as we went to the grocery store, (7) the good supper we ate, (8) the television we enjoyed last evening, (9) another powerful insight I was given during the afternoon, (10) a good night's sleep. That's it. That is what literally happened yesterday and what I thanked the Lord for on this very day. It took just half a minute to thank the Lord for these things.

You don't need to keep a journal; this is just something that I choose to do. But I would urge you to remember to thank the Lord for everything you should be happy about. *Everything.* If you don't keep a journal, then thank him before you go to bed! Don't wait – we all forget so easily! But learn to be thankful and *tell God* what you are thankful for. Don't say to yourself, 'He already knows I'm thankful.' Tell him.

I have come to three conclusions about this matter; when I preach this, I sometimes ask the congregation to repeat these points after me: (1) God loves gratitude; (2) God hates ingratitude; (3) gratitude must be taught.

We used to have a prayer meeting each Sunday before the evening service at Westminster Chapel. It lasted about forty-five minutes. After my own wake-up call in 1988 about being thankful, I felt I should make this a matter of consistent teaching, so I suggested we not put any prayer requests to God until we had spent at least five minutes thanking him for everything. No requests. None. Just petitions of praise.

Having suggested this, we began. Silence. After a minute or two of silence, I said, 'Isn't anybody here thankful about anything?' Silence. I then said, 'Well, thank him for Jesus – will that do?' Then someone prayed, 'We thank you for Jesus.' 'Good,' I said. 'Can someone else thank the Lord for something?' Silence. 'Thank him you are a Christian. Thank him that Jesus died on the cross. Thank him for the Holy Spirit. Thank him for the beautiful weather.' Finally, people got moving. A few weeks later we extended the five minutes to fifteen minutes, and people could hardly wait to utter their own word of thanks for something.

Gratitude must be taught, and that is what I am trying to do in this chapter. When you think to pray, did you think also to thank the Lord?

It is worth mentioning that we are not commanded to thank God *for* everything but *in* everything. 'Give thanks in all circumstances, for this is God's will for you in Christ Jesus' (1 Thess. 5:18). There may be things that happened for which you are not very thankful. I had some things happen yesterday for which I was not particularly thankful:

a large section of my book was accidentally deleted from my computer; I had to re-write it and could not remember all I had written and planned to say; then the computer would not start at all; the weather was the coldest I have experienced in years; we got electricity and gas bills that seemed too high; there is no hint that something rather big I was hoping for will come through – and one or two other things! Am I thankful for all these things? Possibly not. Neither can I tell you honestly that I have remembered to be thankful in all these things as I should.

I only know that God loves gratitude and hates ingratitude, so we must *remember* to be thankful and do our best to tell him. I have written an entire book on this subject (*Thanking God*, Hodder & Stoughton).

Whatever else you thank him for, be sure to thank him for answered prayer. One good reason for having a prayer list is to see how many of those requests can be struck off because he answers! Look over the old prayer list and notice how many of them do not need to be repeated. Never forget to thank him for coming through for you – for protection, for getting you through a difficult situation, for the new friend you wanted, for food, shelter and clothing, for your church, your minister, good worship and singing, good health, a good doctor, friends who will tell you what you need to hear, for good books, for life itself, for spiritual growth, for good entertainment, for knowing all about you and still loving you! You make the list! It will be endless.

Remember: you cannot 'out-thank' the Lord, and you

cannot 'out-give' the Lord (Mal. 3:10; 2 Cor. 9:6ff). When it comes to our showing gratitude, it seems to move him to do all the more for us. As my old friend Michael Leviton used to say, 'God can't stand praise' – he just sends blessings right back to us!

The best way to learn to pray is to interlace each request with as many things you can remember for which you are truly thankful. Don't make him read your mind. Tell him!

9

Practical Matters

I call to you, O LORD, every day. (Ps. 88:9)

A prayer list

In my prayer life, I have not always used a prayer list. I preferred the spontaneity and the feeling of being 'led' by the Spirit as I prayed. It seemed more interesting this way and less tedious.

I have a friend who is a faithful intercessor. He does not use a prayer list; he just waits before the Lord and asks the Holy Spirit to move on him and put people or things on his heart. He assures me that he eventually feels moved to pray for something or someone in particular – and does so with a real burden for them. Often he weeps for them. He believes that he is being heard when he prays in this way, and he feels sure that it is more effective. He does not believe God would put a burden on his heart to pray in this specific manner if God was not also going to hear the same prayer. This makes sense.

Then many years ago, I decided to use a prayer list. The main reason was that I knew I would forget to pray for some people if I didn't use the list. There are certain people I wanted to remember in prayer every day – and there were things I wanted to be sure that I brought to the Lord every day.

Why every day? Because in the most famous parable with regard to prayer, Jesus referred to a widow who 'kept coming' to a judge with a personal request, concluding that we should cry out to God 'day and night' (Luke 18:1–8). You could even make the case that such requests could be mentioned twice a day – 'day and night'. The parable was introduced with a specific purpose – that people 'should always pray and not give up' (Luke 18:1). This clearly implies that we should repeat the same request over and over again.

A prayer list enables us to write down the names of people, their needs and whatever else may be on their hearts and our hearts. The main thing is, we can look at the prayer list as we pray, and linger over each item as we may wish.

Another reason for a prayer list is that it saves time. In the days when I did not have a prayer list, I covered far, far fewer people. In my own experience, I would say I get twenty times more people prayed for – praying for them one by one every day – than I did in the days when I simply prayed as I felt 'led'. There is no way to know whether God is going to answer my prayers for these people when I mention them daily, but neither was there infallible assurance he was hearing me when I prayed as I felt led.

I choose to use categories for my prayer list, one of which is my 'family page'. I begin with the general needs for us all: the daily covering of the blood of Jesus over us – for safety, health, cleansing, fellowship with God and spiritual growth. I pray for the financial needs of family members. Then, beginning with Louise and mentioning each member of our family, I have beside their names specific things they want me to pray for, whether issues with our work situation, people in our lives, unfulfilled desires, material needs, wisdom for a particular decision or situation, and any number of things that pertain to all of us. My requests – hence prayer lists – are very specific, leaving out nothing that I felt was pertinent to our situation.

It is my view that you cannot get too specific in your prayers, and my prayer lists have a lot of details. Why? 'In *all* [my italic] your ways acknowledge him, and he will make your paths straight' (Prov. 3:6). I am so glad God said that! 'All' means *all* and I choose to take this and run with it. There is *no* aspect of my life that is hidden from God, therefore I talk to him about every single, small detail I can think of. If I told some of them to you, you might very well laugh me to scorn. You might even call some of the details on my prayer lists silly or insignificant. They may be silly or insignificant to you, but not to me. Consequently, my prayer lists are sometimes in minute detail, especially for my family. God does not laugh at my requests. At his right hand is our great high priest who is 'touched' with the feeling of my weaknesses (Heb. 4:15 – AV).

My prayer list for Louise and each member of our family includes every aspect of our lives – health, worries, wishes, friends, foes, perspectives, prayer lives, spiritual ambitions, finances, computers, cats, protection, trials, temptations, opportunities, holidays, travel, cars and all other possessions. That is just one page – the family page.

I have a separate page for people I pray for daily. This includes friends, political leaders and those in ministry. In my column for friends I have a list of names, most of whom I merely mention each day. However, with some of them (when they have asked me to) I mention specific things. For those in public ministry I usually mention their names each day (although sometimes I will mention specific things). So too with leaders in government, such as the prime minister of Great Britain and the president of the United States. I prayed for Yasser Arafat every day until he died. I pray for the prime minister of Israel and the Palestinian president. I still pray for the conversion of Osama bin Laden. Why not? As I mentioned earlier, if John Wesley was right, that God does nothing but in answer to prayer, somebody must have been praying for Saul of Tarsus (no mean terrorist). We should pray for everybody in public life whenever we can. My wife Louise began praying for Nelson Mandela every day over thirty years ago – and still prays for him daily. I have prayed for Her Majesty the Queen daily for well over thirty years.

One should perhaps have another section on political matters, world peace, alarming trends and the condition of the Church. For over thirty years I have prayed publicly and privately for peace in the Middle East and the peace of Jerusalem. I have prayed for revival in the Church for as long as I can remember.

I have yet another page for my own spiritual needs and desires: for an ever-increasing anointing and insight; wisdom as to the next book – and wisdom while writing the current book; that I will know when to say yes and when to say no when invited somewhere; that God will determine whom I meet; that I will continue to forgive totally those who have hurt me (some I have had to pray regularly for – that God will bless them – to prove I mean it!). Another section on this page comprises the theological and biblical questions I have. Do you have theological questions? Are there verses in the Bible you don't understand? I have them too. Which ones? I will let you guess. But there are a good number of verses that remain a mystery to me. There are a lot of theological issues that are not as clear to me as I would like – and I keep praying that God will clarify these matters to me.

There are verses I *read* every day in addition to my Bible reading plan. I know most of them by heart, but I read them anyway – it is good discipline. Besides, I often have the Spirit quicken me in a surprising way when I read some of these verses. I will share some of them with you: Luke 6:37 (my greatest weakness is wanting to point the finger, so I read this one every day – that I won't judge); Ephesians 5:25–33 (that I will be a better husband), and Philippians 4:4–6 (I need all the help I can get to remember to rejoice, be gentle and not be anxious).

For that deacon who said, 'I don't know what to say after praying for five minutes' – or whoever else might say this – I hope I have shown that you can fill thirty minutes or more a day with little difficulty if you have a prayer list.

As for praying in the style of my friend who intercedes as he feels led, I reply further: why not do this too? Surely you can have it both ways on this – if you have the time. If I devote my time only to praying as I feel led, it will mean that an awful lot of people probably won't get prayed for. But if I have a prayer list – to make sure certain people get mentioned daily – I can always take as many moments as I choose to ask the Holy Spirit to bring people or situations to my mind.

I will never forget (and can't repeat it too often) how Louise used to chide me for asking my church members to pray for thirty minutes a day. But one day she was touched quite supernaturally by the Holy Spirit through the ministry of Rodney Howard-Browne. One of the immediate results was that she wanted to pray two hours a day – if only she had the time! That desire has never left her.

If someone should say to me that I am bordering on displaying my righteousness before people (cf. Matt. 6:5ff) by talking about time in prayer, and how we do it, I can understand that. I don't blame anybody for their thoughts along this line. All I can say is, if these lines can inspire you to pray more, I gladly forfeit any reward in heaven. I am not trying to make you think I am super-pious (I certainly am not), but I honestly aspire to motivate all my readers to pray more than ever. I am glad to know that people like John Wesley and Martin Luther prayed two hours every day. This inspires me. That is all I want – to inspire you to pray and pray more. Praying is not wasted time. There will be no praying in heaven. Pray now. As much as you can. You will not be sorry. And I recommend a prayer list.

Posture

When I was growing up I mostly knew one posture in praying – kneeling. We did it at home; we did it at church. You will recall my earliest memory of my father – on his knees every morning before he went to work. My mother always knelt to pray in her quiet time, but we always stood when she prayed with me before I went to school.

My dad called it our 'family altar'. This took place on Sunday mornings before church and each evening. After one of us read several verses from the Bible (we took turns), my mother, father and I each knelt around the dining room table and prayed before going to bed. Never once do I recall sitting to pray at home.

My quiet time as a teenager found me on my knees before my rocking chair each morning and every night. I also read several verses from the Bible. I usually sat to read; I knelt when praying.

At my Nazarene church in Ashland, Kentucky, we would usually stand to pray on Sunday mornings, but always knelt on Sunday evenings. Nearly every person present knelt to pray. We did not have a kneeling pad or rail on which to kneel forwards; we would turn around, kneel and face the back of the pew. It was normal for everybody to pray out loud simultaneously when the congregation prayed on Sunday evenings. The person who led in prayer, not always the pastor, would have to raise his voice to be heard, and often would *not* be heard except when he started and just before he finished.

When I left home, for some reason I began sitting to pray. After Louise and I married we did pray while kneeling for a while, but later we began to sit to pray. When my father would visit us and we would have a time of family prayer, he would go on to his knees – so we all joined him. He could not imagine praying any other way. When we visited his house, we always knelt to pray.

For the whole of my adult life I have made it a practice to sit when praying. I don't know why, I just chose to sit (and didn't feel guilty). When I used to visit Dr Martyn Lloyd-Jones on Thursdays we would pray together –

always sitting. When an old Nazarene friend, Spencer Johnson, visited me in my vestry at Westminster Chapel, he got on his knees when I suggested we pray. I did the same thing with him of course. When I was in my darkest hour at Westminster Chapel I visited my Oxford University supervisor, Dr Barrie White. The only time I saw him pray on his knees was that day; he was feeling my burden and I always appreciated his doing that.

If you look for a biblical basis for posture in prayer, you will find support for any position. The most prominent posture, however, was kneeling. This is because it showed humility and reverence to God. 'Come, let us bow down in worship, let us kneel before the LORD our Maker' (Ps. 95:6).

The first reference to posture and prayer in the Bible is when Solomon prayed to dedicate the temple. When he finished praying 'he rose from before the altar of the LORD, where he had been kneeling with his hands spread out towards heaven' (1 Kgs. 8:54). The parallel description of the same event says that Solomon stood on the platform 'and then knelt down before the whole assembly of Israel and spread out his hands towards heaven' (2 Chron. 6:13). Daniel knelt when he prayed. 'Three times a day he got down on his knees and prayed, giving thanks to his God, just as he had done before' (Dan. 6:10). Elijah was probably kneeling 'when he bent to the ground and put his face between his knees' (1 Kgs. 18:42), although some believe he was sitting on the ground. On at least one occasion, Ezra knelt to pray (Ezra 9:5).

Jesus knelt when he prayed in the Garden of Gethsemane (Luke 22:41). Stephen fell to his knees to pray for his persecutors just before he died (Acts 7:60). Just before Peter raised Tabitha from the dead, he 'got down on his knees and prayed' (Acts 9:40). Just before Paul said goodbye to the elders at Ephesus 'he knelt down with all of them and prayed' (Acts 20:36). Luke records an occasion when on the beach 'we knelt to pray' (Acts 21:5). Paul said, 'I kneel before the Father' as he prayed for the Ephesians (Eph. 3:14).

The Pharisees apparently stood to pray, 'standing in the synagogues and on the street corners to be seen by men' (Matt. 6:5; cf. Luke 18:11). The priests who ministered in the ancient times did so standing (Num. 11:16; 16:9; Deut. 10:8; cf. Ps. 134:1 (AV) and Ps. 135:2 (AV); 2 Chron. 5:14).

The most desperate position for praying was signified by lying prostrate on the ground, probably face down. When the outlook was the bleakest, this is what people some-times did. This was David's posture following his exposure by Nathan the prophet after Nathan told him the child from his adulterous relationship with Bathsheba would die. He pleaded with God for the child's life. David fasted and 'spent the nights lying on the ground' (2 Sam. 12:16). When David later received the news that Absalom killed Amnon, he 'tore his clothes and lay down on the ground' (2 Sam. 13:31). Have you ever been so desperate that you only wanted to lie face down on the floor?

I know of only one example of a person sitting to pray

in the Bible. This was when David had been told by Nathan the prophet that he would not be allowed to build the temple. 'King David went in and sat before the LORD' and prayed (2 Sam. 7:18). That is a pretty good example for sitting to pray if you ask me.

And yet there *is* another example of a person sitting to pray! Our Lord Jesus Christ, our great high priest, is now sitting at God's right hand making intercession for us (Heb. 1:3; 7:25). You could argue that the most effectual praying of all is done by one sitting!

I have also spent a lot of time walking and praying, and I have a friend who prays when he jogs. I am sure you can ride a bicycle and pray, and you can certainly drive and pray. Some of my greatest experiences with the Lord have come while I was driving.

The truth is that it does not matter what posture describes you in your prayer life. The main thing is your answer to the question, 'Did you think to pray?' Sitting, kneeling, jogging, standing or lying on the floor, be sure you remember to spend time with God alone.

Closing your eyes to pray

'Please bow your head and close your eyes,' the evangelist will sometimes say to his congregation. This is probably to keep people from looking around just before the altar call is given.

Some of us were taught to close our eyes when we pray. There is nothing wrong with this, but I can find no biblical basis for closing your eyes when you pray. Jesus didn't close his eyes when he prayed, as far as we can tell. On at least two occasions Jesus prayed with his eyes wide open. 'Jesus looked up and said, "Father, I thank you that you have heard me" ' (John 11:41). The Greek says he lifted up his eyes, as in John 17:1: 'He looked towards heaven and prayed.'

The only reason I can think of for closing your eyes is to avoid distraction. So this is a good reason to close your eyes. I think too it shows respect when you close your eyes when public prayer is being offered.

The best time to pray

When as a young Christian I happened to read that Jesus prayed in the morning, I thought that was the best time to pray – to follow Jesus' example. 'Very early in the morning, while it was still dark, Jesus got up, left the house and went off to a solitary place, where he prayed' (Mark 1:35). But I later read that on another occasion he went up on a mountainside 'by himself to pray. When evening came, he was there alone' (Matt. 14:23). If we had only Mark's account, we would say Jesus had quiet times in the mornings. If we only had Matthew's account, we could conclude he prayed in the evenings. But if we had only

Luke's account we might think he spent every night – all night long – in prayer. 'One of those days Jesus went out to a mountainside to pray, and spent the night praying to God' (Luke 6:12).

When should you pray? There is a simple answer: when it is best and easiest for you. I myself am more of a 'morning' person than nocturnal. I therefore prefer mornings for my own quiet time. But there are those who have so much trouble waking up most mornings (even with strong tea or coffee) that they would waste their quiet time by trying to read the Bible and pray then. There are those who 'come alive' in the evenings. If this describes you, I would advise you to have your quiet time in the evenings.

During my time in London when I urged Westminster Chapel members to spend 30 minutes a day in prayer, I learned of one dear man who had to get up at 5 a.m. each day to get to work by 7 a.m. because of the location of his job and because of the public transport situation. He wondered if he could use the time on the train to do his quiet time? Of course! The last thing I want to do is to superimpose bondage and legalism! I am not writing this book to make people feel guilty or to give you an unrealistic standard. 'God does not oppress us,' Dr Lloyd-Jones used to say to me. I write this book to encourage you to do what you *want* to do, not what you are unable to do!

If I had to pick my favourite verse in any psalm it is this: 'For he [God] knows how we are formed, he remembers that we are dust' (Ps. 103:14).

Pray as much as you can, as often as you can, as best as you can for as long as you can. Learn all you can about prayer. Then know that God enjoys your company and will take all he can get when it comes to your spending time with him.

PART FOUR

Advanced Lessons In Prayer

10

The Sacrifice of Praise

Through Jesus, therefore, let us continually
offer to God a sacrifice of praise – the fruit of
lips that confess his name. (Heb. 13:15)

Would you be willing to go with me on an extended journey? By that I mean going deeper into this matter of prayer.

If I were to suggest that what I have taught up to now in this book is 'milk', what would you say? That what I have written so far are basic, elementary lessons on the subject of prayer.

There is nothing wrong with milk. We all need it, especially as we are growing up, but eventually we need to eat meat or solid food.

The Apostle Paul said to his beloved Corinthians: 'I gave you milk, not solid food, for you were not ready for it'

(1 Cor. 3:2). The writer of the Epistle to the Hebrews scolded these Jewish Christians, 'By this time you ought to be teachers, you need someone to teach you the elementary truths of God's word all over again. You need milk, not solid food! Anyone who lives on milk, being still an infant, is not acquainted with the teaching about righteousness. But solid food is for the mature, who by constant use have trained themselves to distinguish good from evil' (Heb. 5:12–14).

I have sought to write this book as if the reader knows little or nothing about prayer. This way, nobody is left out. But I also want to try to lead everyone from 'school' to 'university' when it comes to prayer, although I am not sure that I myself am there. Perhaps it comes when you cross over a line, even though you are not initially aware you did. This happened to Jacob. He wrestled with God, not knowing at first that this was what he was doing. He thought he was wrestling with an enemy, but at some point realised this man he was confronted with was a friend – yes, more than a friend. Jacob said to him, 'I will not let you go unless you bless me.' This is when Jacob was given the name Israel, 'because you have struggled with God and with men and have overcome' (Gen. 32:28). I love the Authorised Version: 'as a prince hast thou power with God and with men, and hast prevailed'.

There is no 'gift of prayer' in the list of the spiritual gifts in 1 Corinthians 12:8–10 or in Romans 12:6–8. The reason is probably because we are all on level ground when it comes to prayer. Not all of us can have the talent or spiritual gifts we may wish for; they are sovereignly given (Rom. 12:3; 1 Cor. 12:11). But all of us can pray, and all of us can excel in prayer. Indeed, 'the prayer of a righteous man is powerful and effective' (James 5:16). But if that adjective 'righteous' is as threatening to you as it is to me, take heart; James followed this with a reference to Elijah as 'a man just like us' (James 5:17 – 'a man subject to like passions as we are' (AV)). Elijah was as human as you get, but through it all had some of the most extraordinary answers to prayer in all the Bible (James 5:17–18; 1 Kgs. 17–19).

I find this so encouraging. Nobody is given a supernatural ability or private gift to excel in this matter of prayer, and yet anybody can pray and see great answers to prayer. God invites ordinary people to experience the supernatural.

Furthermore, I do not say you have to enter 'university' to do this. Jennifer Rees Larcombe is a legendary Christian woman in Britain. I first met her when she was paralysed and sitting in a wheelchair. The next time I saw her she was walking around as if she had not been paralysed all those years. She had many people, some with a high profile, to lay their hands on her for healing. But the actual healing came when a young lady who had been converted only two weeks before prayed for her!

On the other hand, I think we need to grow in the knowledge of prayer. This is what I want to emphasise in

Part Four, 'Advanced Lessons in Prayer'. I want to learn all I can about prayer and I am going to share everything I know so far, holding back nothing.

One of the first steps we must take in this move from milk to solid food is the matter of praise in prayer. We have already had a chapter on gratitude, but praise in prayer is a step further, as we will see. With thankfulness you only need to remember to say thanks; with praise you not only need to remember, but to sacrifice. It may mean work.

In my opinion, praising God in prayer is one of the hardest things we are commanded to do because praise does not come easily. It takes discipline, will-power, concentration. It does not come naturally. And yet we have to make a choice to do it. Doing so seems as if it is done in our own strength – as a matter of fact, so much growth in the Christian life seems as if it is in our own strength. But later on we see that what we did was through the Spirit. And I can tell you, if you make the decision to praise God in prayer, it is the Spirit and not the flesh at work! The flesh will *never* move your heart to spend time praising the Lord.

This is why the Bible refers to the 'sacrifice of praise'. Yes, praising God is a sacrifice on our part.

And yet I have been surprised that the Bible admits that praising God is a sacrifice. In other words, this phrase is an explicit recognition that praising God isn't easy to do.

To me, then, it shows amazing candour for the writer of the Epistle to the Hebrews to call praising God a sacrifice. But I believe it! Referring to a 'sacrifice of praise' is saying what I have personally *felt*, but felt guilty thinking – namely, that it *is* an effort, a sacrifice, to take time to praise God.

It shouldn't be a sacrifice, but it is. I should be so grateful that God has done so much for me that I exude praise all the time. If only . . .

Now if I am feeling a little pious, I may not regard praising God as much of a sacrifice. If I am in a good mood (a less frequent occurrence than I care for you to know) or I am feeling spiritual (which is rarer than I care for you to know), perhaps I would *not* call praising God a sacrifice. But my personal experience is that praising God usually requires effort.

So even the Bible calls praising God a 'sacrifice'. This word may be understood in two ways. First, in the Epistle to the Hebrews, its primary usage refers to the shedding of blood of an animal. The sacrificial system in the Old Testament was inextricably linked to atonement. Without the shedding of blood there is no remission for sins (Heb. 9:22). Much of this epistle refers to atonement and sacrifice.

But at the end of the Epistle to the Hebrews the writer uses the word 'sacrifice' in a different way. Here, the word means our giving up something *valued* for the sake of praising the Lord.

So what is it that is *valued* that we set aside? First, our time. We sacrifice time. We never get that time back. You sacrifice moments you might have used for important projects. As for praising God in prayer, you might have preferred to spend the time putting your requests to God. It is easier to ask for things than merely to praise God. You will recall how I led the people of Westminster Chapel to do nothing but thank God for a few moments.

You will ask: is not thanking God and praising God the same thing? No. Thanking God is showing gratitude for what he has *done*; praising God is affirming him for what and who he *is*. Yes, you can certainly praise God for what he has done. But I speak now of just praising the Lord for his being *just like he is*. He likes that.

The most thrilling thing a husband or wife can hear from their spouse is, 'I love you for being who you are and just like you are.' It doesn't get better than that.

You may say: 'But I am not sure I like everything about God.'

I reply: this is why we must move from the 'school' of prayer to the 'university' of the Holy Spirit. This is going from milk to solid food. You may not get there overnight; it may take a while.

I remember hearing a man pray in a church many years ago in the mountains of Tennessee. He said something I had never heard before and I am not sure I have heard it since. He was not referring to the world situation, but things in his own personal life when he was under considerable stress: 'Lord, I thank you that everything is just like it is and that you are just like you are.' Wow. Have you ever said that to God before? Could you?

I cannot say you should be doing this too – at least at this moment. I am not sure you are required to praise God for everything being just like it is. I don't even want to go much more into this here, only to say that you may *eventually* praise God for the situation you found unbearable at the time. After all, all things do indeed work together for good to them that love God, to those who are called according to his purpose (Rom. 8:28).

It was one of Job's finest moments when he exclaimed, 'Though he slay me, yet will I trust him' (Job 13:15 – AV). When you can affirm God in your darkest hour – and when nothing makes sense – you bring him great glory and honour and praise.

It is the highest devotion to praise God for being just as he is. And if you cannot do this now, I pray you will soon be able to do so.

What you and I *should* do now, however, is to keep praising God, whether we feel like it or not – otherwise, praising God is no sacrifice. The point is that you don't wait until you are 'led'; you do it because it is right.

There is something that Louise and I do fairly regularly – we try to do it every day – and that is singing and praying together. We use a hymn book or chorus book and sing together for around ten minutes – then pray together.

I must now tell you something that happened as I was preparing to write this very chapter on 'The Sacrifice of Praise'. As I began, all my thoughts completely left me. Every writer knows what this is like. It is something we all dread. It was now happening to me. I waited for the inspiration. Nothing came. I prayed. There was nothing. I looked out of our window on lovely Hickory Lake where we now live near Nashville. It is gorgeous, but I got no word worth writing. No clear thoughts came. None. In the meantime, Louise called to me, 'Do you want to sing and pray?' I was not blessed by the suggestion, and inwardly I sighed. To be honest, I was annoyed. Why hadn't she suggested this earlier this morning, I thought. Something had come up and we hadn't managed to pray together yet. I was behind in writing and I had a lot to do. 'I need to work on this chapter,' I said to her. 'Maybe later.'

Then I realised the irony and hypocrisy of it all and, thankfully, began to feel ashamed. Here I was trying to write a chapter on 'The Sacrifice of Praise' and the precise moment Louise asks me to praise God with her, I rebel at the thought. How hypocritical can one be? I then begrudgingly said, 'OK, let's do it.' I didn't have the courage to tell her the very title of this chapter I was trying to write. And yet taking time to sing and pray at that moment was a sacrifice I simply didn't want to make. But I eventually said, 'OK, let's sing and pray now.' We did. I felt no great joy in doing it, however. But we sang for ten minutes and then went through several items on our prayer lists. Then I went back to my computer.

And what do you suppose happened? Surprise, surprise. When I returned to write, the ideas for this chapter began to pour into my heart like water from a burst dam. The thoughts came more quickly than I was able to type.

It all goes to show that you cannot 'out-praise' God. I learned something from this. God held no grudges for my temporary rebellion. So in this incident today, even when I praised him with a negative spirit, God chose to bless me. He really did.

And yet I know of no *explicit* promise in the Bible that states 'you will be blessed if you take time to praise God'. The nearest to this are words that hint very strongly that praise brings blessing. For example, 'May the peoples praise you, O God; may all the peoples praise you. *Then* the land will yield its harvest, and God, our God, will bless us' (emphasis mine, Ps. 67:5–6). But possibly the most powerful example of this is when the people of Judah were outnumbered and on the verge of being defeated in a major battle. What follows speaks for itself:

> *Jehoshaphat appointed men to sing to the* LORD *and to praise him for the splendour of his holiness as they went out at the head of the army, saying: 'Give thanks to the* LORD, *for his love endures for ever.' As they began to sing and praise, the* LORD *set ambushes against the men of Ammon and Moab and Mount Seir who were invading Judah, and they were defeated.* (2 Chron. 20:21–22)

As the psalmist put it, 'But thou art holy, O thou that inhabitest the praises of Israel' (Ps. 22:3 – AV). If God inhabits our praise, then that is a pretty good reason to praise him if getting close to him is what you want!

It is true: you cannot 'out-give' the Lord, you cannot 'out-thank' the Lord, you cannot 'out-praise' the Lord.

And yet I still feel that it was very gracious of the writer of the Epistle to the Hebrews – hence the Lord – to call praising God a *sacrifice* on our part. Jesus is touched with the feeling of our weaknesses (Heb. 4:15) and our Father remembers we are dust (Ps. 103:14). Whereas taking the time to praise him is what we as his children ought always to do – whether we feel like it or not – he stoops to our weakness and lets us know that he realises it is a sacrifice on our part when we take time to praise him.

Ashamed as I was in this matter of not wanting to leave my computer to pray and sing with Louise, I did not feel scolded by the Lord, I did not feel moralised. He was, simply, being gracious.

It is therefore called a 'sacrifice of praise' because we forfeit time that we will never get back. I am late in getting this book to my publisher, and signed a contract that stated I would have this manuscript in their hands a week ago. I needed all the time I could find to get this book written. To stop and pray and sing with Louise required time I needed for writing – but how wrong I was in trying to justify my feelings.

It is called 'sacrifice of praise' also because it goes right against nature. It is *natural* to want to watch television, to eat, to sleep, to read a newspaper, to listen to music – or even to ask God for things. Everybody prays when they are in trouble. General Douglas MacArthur used to say 'there are no atheists in foxholes (trenches)'. Therefore calling on God when you are desperate has a natural explanation, but praising God whether you feel like it or not goes against the natural grain of our souls.

The same thing could be said for *learning* to praise God. Thankfulness and praise often overlap, but praising God, as we have seen, is taking thankfulness a step further. And I would have to say that learning to praise indicates a much more mature level of faith and practice. That is why this chapter is not near the beginning of the book. This phrase 'sacrifice of praise' was addressed to discouraged, somewhat backslidden, Hebrew Christians.

Just as gratitude must be taught, so too must we learn to praise God. We were actually introduced to this in the Lord's Prayer. When we say 'hallowed be your name', we are praising God.

But we ought to learn to do more than merely say those words. Praising God in prayer is affirming God for being *God*, for having a will of his own and a mind of his own. It is not merely thanking him for things; it is telling him how much you like what he does and what he is like. When you feel the opposite but praise him just the same, you are going right against nature; you cross over into the supernatural. You become like Jacob – you prevail. God wants that for us.

When you realise that these words 'sacrifice of praise'

were given to discouraged, somewhat backslidden Christians, you wonder what their reaction might be to words like that! Discouraged people don't readily respond to the idea of praising God when things aren't so good and when God doesn't make sense. And yet that is exactly what the writer said to them.

Dr Martyn Lloyd-Jones used to say that 'a discouraged church doesn't need comfort, it needs doctrine'. There is no stronger teaching than learning to praise God when you don't feel like doing it. It is a transition from 'milk' to 'meat'.

Praising God is both a privilege and a duty.

And yet what we give up in our sacrifice of praise is either temporary or compensated for many times over. The truth is, ultimately we do not give up anything. We get much more back.

But that is not the reason to do it. We should not give to get, neither should we praise God to receive more. We praise him because he deserves it. We praise him because he is worthy. We praise him because we are eternally indebted to having a God like he is.

Let me offer some suggestions on how to praise God in prayer.

Read those psalms that extol God for his goodness and mercy. Ask yourself: how did the psalmist know to talk to God like that? Why don't you and I do the same thing? We have an advantage over the psalmist: since the psalms were written, Jesus has come, died and risen from the dead; the

Holy Spirit has fallen on the Church; we have the entire Bible – Old and New Testaments. If the psalmist could praise God as he did, you and I should be able to do it even better.

Get an old hymn book and start reading the hymns. Better still, sing them. Sing hymns that you have never heard of before; sing those that you *have* heard of – 'All hail the power of Jesus' Name', 'I'll praise my maker while I've breath', 'Praise my soul the King of heaven', 'And can it be that I should gain an interest in the Saviour's blood?'

Find a contemporary hymn or praise book and sing the hymns and choruses. Great music and poetry are still being composed and written today.

Try talking to God from your heart by telling him what you like about him. In the same way we count our blessings of the previous day, and tell the Lord, so too we praise him for his *ways*. The more time you spend with the Lord, the more you experience and are aware of his 'ways'. God lamented of ancient Israel, 'They have not known my *ways*' (emphasis mine, Heb. 3:10). Moses wanted to learn about God's 'ways' (Exod. 33:13). As you begin to learn his ways, praise him for those ways!

The thing is, God is a God of glory. He is a jealous God (Exod. 34:14). Being jealous is not a happy human trait. But like it or not, that is the way God is! Praise him for being jealous. It is because of his jealousy that you are kept safe! It is in your keenest interest that he is a jealous God. He loves you so much, he looks after you all the time.

Praise him for his attributes – his power, his infinite knowledge, his omnipresence, his sovereignty, his holiness, his love, his tenderness.

The truth is, in our fallen state, praise is not a natural phenomenon, but the rewards are immense. Do you want to cross over into the supernatural? Then just praise the Lord.

By the way, the best time to do it is when you are at your lowest – that is when you *really* go against human nature. Don't wait until you feel like doing it. The consummate victory is to those who struggle to do it. When you prevail over the enemy as Jacob did, you find your best friend. There is no better way to begin than by starting to praise God, whatever the circumstances. Do it now.

11

Did You Think to Fast?

> When you fast, do not look sombre as the
> hypocrites do, for they disfigure their faces to
> show men they are fasting. I tell you the truth,
> they have received their reward in full.
>
> (Matt. 6:16)

When God is hiding his face, when the burden you are carrying seems almost unbearable, when nothing seems to be going right and everything seems wrong – and even God doesn't make sense – what do you do?

Did you think to fast?

What if you are truly, earnestly and eagerly wanting a closer walk with God – and seem to be making no progress?

Did you think to fast?

Could it be that fasting is the next step forward for you?

Fasting is a godly inconvenience we impose on ourselves

voluntarily when we feel it is the only thing to do. It should not be done every day, neither should it be carried out as a perfunctory thing. Choosing to fast is the right decision when you are left with no other choice – because you urgently need to hear from God or have him step in.

The purpose of fasting is basically twofold: (1) when you need urgently to see God work, and (2) when you are trying to get God's attention. Sometimes, however, people in ancient times fasted as a sign of mourning (1 Sam. 1:13; 2 Sam. 1:12). Fasting is not an end in itself; it is the means that God sometimes honours when our motive is to get him to reveal his glory and take notice of our plight. He already knows everything of course, and loves us with an everlasting love (Jer. 31:3), but we will see in this chapter that people fasted none the less in order to know for sure that God was truly with them, to get his attention and see him work.

Fasting means total abstinence from food, not water. To go without water is dangerous; to go without food can be healthy. Some people actually fast for physical reasons, but that is not what this chapter is about.

I write now about going without food for *spiritual* reasons: you do it because you are trying to get God's attention. When the ancient Israelites said, 'Why have we fasted . . . and you have not seen it? Why have we humbled ourselves, and you have not noticed?' (Isa. 58:3) it reveals what ancient Israel regarded as the main purpose of fasting – to get God to take notice. The hope is, God will see how desperate we are and take pity on us. That is the point.

We fast from eating food because it is a way of depriving ourselves of something we enjoy. Like praising God (as we saw in the previous chapter), fasting too is a sacrifice. Fasting is not meant to be fun. We therefore give up something enjoyable as evidence of how earnest we are to hear from God and show we need his blessing. It is our small way of trying to declare to God, 'See, now do you believe I am earnest about this matter?'

Private fasting for spiritual reasons pleases God if he is the only one who knows about it. The Pharisees got no satisfaction from fasting if people did not know they were fasting. They lived for adulation, especially that people would think they were very pious. That was *so* important to them. As Jesus said, 'Everything they do is done for men to see' (Matt. 23:5). Jesus therefore counsels you and me to hide the fact that we are fasting – to let nobody but God know. This way, we will honour him and receive the reward that comes from him only (John 5:44). Jesus thus said, 'Put oil on your head and wash your face' (Matt. 6:17). By this he simply means to brush or comb your hair, dress as you normally would, and keep the fact that you are fasting a secret from those around you.

When I was twelve, I read this passage about going into your closet and shutting the door when you pray (Matt. 6:6 – AV) and anointing your head when you fast. So I did that. I got some oil and put it on my head. Then I walked into the same cupboard where I hung my clothes – and shut the door. It was totally dark. I felt nothing. I stayed in the dark cupboard for a minute or two, then came out, feeling a little disappointed that God hadn't shown up. I never did that again. Of course, I later learned the true meaning of this passage. And yet I like to think that waiting on the Lord in my dark cupboard sixty years ago with oil on my head did me no harm – that God even smiled on me for my wanting to get it right.

God wants us to fast and pray if our only motive is to seek his face. It is not to impress God that you are righteous. And yet it became a way to score points with God – impressing him with how holy they were – for the ancient Pharisees. In one of his parables Jesus spoke about the Pharisee who believed he was righteous, partly because he fasted twice a week (Luke 18:12). But Jesus gave no hint that fasting counted for righteousness. He did, however, promise that there was a reward for fasting. If you fast before God alone and do not tell people, 'your Father, who sees what is done in secret, will reward you' (Matt. 6:18). Jesus thus stressed that if our motive for fasting is to cause people to admire us, we forfeit the reward that would have come to us. If their knowing we fast is what gives us pleasure, then the praise of people will be the only reward we get.

Public fasting, however, is rather different; a church can decide to fast corporately and obviously this will not be kept secret. The early Church did this: 'While they were worshipping the Lord and fasting, the Holy Spirit said, "Set apart for me Barnabas and Saul for the work to which I have called them." So after they had fasted and prayed, they placed their hands on them and sent them off' (Acts 13:2–3). When a church fasts corporately, it will be done as a family – hopefully not to impress one another, although the pride of the human heart is ever at hand.

There is never a guarantee that fasting will achieve what we want, and this must never be forgotten. If fasting always worked, people would fast all the time! God is sovereign. His word to Moses, 'I will have mercy on whom I will have mercy, and I will have compassion on whom I will have compassion' (Exod. 33:19), has not changed. What increases the agony in fasting is our *not* knowing for sure whether it will achieve its goal.

So, like it or not, we fast with the understanding that it may not necessarily achieve what we hope for. You cannot control God. Indeed, David, a man after God's own heart, fasted over his child's illness, hoping God would change his mind and spare the child. But the child died.

And yet Jesus assumed we would fast. He did not say 'if' you fast, but 'when'. 'When you fast, do not look sombre as the hypocrites do, for they disfigure their faces to show men they are fasting.' Isn't that amazing? To think that what used to be the means to get *God's* attention had degenerated into the means to get *people's* attention! In saying 'when' you fast, Jesus did not mean for us to carry this out *except* to seek God's face, but he was none the less·

condoning fasting as an acceptable means to seek the Lord when this practice seems the only way forward.

And Jesus knew there *would* be times when fasting would be the only way forward. The word 'when' shows he expects us to have times like that. 'In this world you will have trouble,' Jesus said (John 16:33).

The disciples of John the Baptist were puzzled that Jesus' disciples did not fast. After all, John the Baptist's disciples fasted; the Pharisees fasted. Why, they argued, not Jesus' disciples? Jesus' answer was very simple. Why should his disciples fast when they have Jesus himself right there with them? The reason you fast is because God is hiding his face. He seems absent. It would appear he is looking the other way, so you fast to try to get God's attention! But Jesus' disciples *had* his attention, hence there was no need to fast. However, Jesus said, that will change one day: 'The time will come when the bridegroom [Jesus] will be taken from them [when he would ascend to heaven]; then they will fast' (Matt. 9:15).

Therefore in the early Church the followers of Jesus fasted. In other words, now that Jesus was in heaven – and when things weren't going too well – they tried fasting. I would assume that it was when the Lord's presence was not so manifest that the early Church fasted. When the power of God is manifest to a high level, I can't imagine the Church fasting. Nobody was fasting on the day of Pentecost, but there were times when the sense of God diminished. This is apparently what was happening when they worshipped the

Lord – and fasted. One thing is certain: God honoured that fast! While they were fasting, the Holy Spirit spoke powerfully, 'Set apart for me Barnabas and Saul for the work to which I have called them.'

It would seem that the first precedent for fasting was that of Moses when he was forty days on the mountain at Horeb: 'When I went up on the mountain to receive the tablets of stone, the tablets of the covenant that the LORD had made with you, I stayed on the mountain forty days and forty nights; I ate no bread and drank no water' (Deut. 9:9; cf. Exod. 34:28). Fasting without water for forty days would result in death, so Moses must have had supernatural care in this fast. Jesus too went on a forty-day fast (Matt. 4:1ff). You and I should never be so foolish as to expect that God would enable us to fast for longer than a couple of days without water.

However, I happen to know that when a certain church in Kenya fasts for two weeks every January, the people assume they will neither eat nor drink during this time. I will not try to explain that, only to say I would not advise this. When we fasted as a church at Westminster Chapel, I always urged people to drink lots of water, even though it was only fasting for one day. But it could have been my lack of faith – or fear of people becoming ill – that lay behind my caution.

Fasting was commanded on the Day of Atonement (Lev. 16:29), but the practice later on came to be voluntary, especially when the people of Israel sought help from God

(Judges 20:26; 1 Sam. 14:24). When Samuel realised how Israel had sinned, he called all the people together: 'On that day they fasted and there they confessed, "We have sinned against the LORD" ' (1 Sam. 7:6). When Jehoshaphat was told, 'A vast army is coming against you,' he 'proclaimed a fast for all Judah' (2 Chron. 20:2–3). When Ezra needed unusual protection, 'We fasted and petitioned our God about this, and he answered our prayer' (Ezra 8:23). God himself required the people on another occasion to fast. ' "Even now," declares the LORD, "return to me with all your heart, with fasting and weeping and mourning" ' (Joel 2:12). A sign that revival was coming to Nineveh after Jonah's preaching was that the king declared a fast (Jonah 3:5).

Sadly, fasting eventually became an outward basis of showing piety. For some it was a work of merit. And yet, as we have seen, rather than discontinue the practice, Jesus assumed that it would continue. He simply gave instructions and warned that it would have no value whatsoever unless God put his seal on the fast, and that this was only done when God was sought without a person feeling righteous for doing it. Indeed, in the context of giving, praying and fasting, there was this underlying caution: 'Do not let your left hand know what your right hand is doing' (Matt. 6:3). This means that there is a sense in which we don't even tell ourselves that we are giving, praying or fasting; it is not to be a self-conscious matter whereby we feel we are doing something great.

Fasting therefore carries with it a danger of letting us take ourselves too seriously. This is why we must not only *not* tell others; we shouldn't let ourselves think about it, if possible.

We must learn not only *not* to expect too much from fasting, we should not be too disappointed if we *feel* nothing during the fast.

I have experienced it both ways. I have known times when God *did* show up during the time of a fast, but I have had more times when he did not intervene – in so far as any conscious awareness was concerned anyway. The answer tended to come later.

Spurgeon once put it like this: I looked to Christ and the Dove flew in, I looked to the Dove and he disappeared. This means we should turn to the Lord Jesus when we are fasting and not look for any immediate results from it. The problem is, if we *do* see immediate results, we will start expecting them every time – and not look to the Lord as we should.

Any fasting we do, then, should be done by seeking God's face without any feeling that we are doing something pious or that he will necessarily step in as we wish or as soon as we wish.

What kind of reward might come from our heavenly Father if we fast in secret? First, if we truly do it before him and do it for his honour, we can be assured that we are pleasing him. There is no greater reward than knowing you please the Lord. And when you seek his face in fasting without any thought other than his glory, this pleases him. In other words, knowing you please him is reward enough.

Second, God may manifest himself in unexpected ways. This happened to me the first time we fasted as a church at Westminster Chapel. To my great surprise, God spoke to me in a most unusual way that day, and I was not prepared for it. We fasted corporately. We wanted to be grateful for our unity and ask God for his greater blessing for the coming year. I was not expecting anything to come to me personally, but it did.

The following year, however, when we had a day of prayer and fasting again – and I found myself expecting a repeat of what had happened the first time – *nothing whatever* came to me personally. It was a long, boring day and I felt starved. Never did breakfast the next morning taste so good.

Third, the blessing of God may come further down the road. In other words, the very thing you ask for may be answered – months or even years later. You therefore go through the day without food, praying as much as you can. In those days we would meet as a church in the evening for those who could come. Not all who fasted could join us at the church. But we would meet for two hours to pray and worship. They were precious days. We would have no idea on the day or evening itself whether God would hear our prayers of that particular day. And yet I have no doubt that these prayers were heard and that the fasting was blessed.

Not that the genuine revival we all prayed for came; but they were sweet days of unity and blessing.

When our family were on vacation in the summer of 1984, our church was in a deep crisis and the unity was being torn apart. It all began when I started the Pilot Light ministry in the streets of Victoria, began giving altar calls, and singing choruses (not just hymns). Six of the twelve deacons turned the issue into a theological one. I knew in my heart that what was at stake had nothing to do with what I taught regarding doctrine; it was breaking with cherished traditions that was at the root of the trouble. That summer in Key Largo, Florida, I set aside three days to fast. I did no fishing, I ate no food, drank only water. During the fast, I felt nothing. When we recommenced our ministry in September, the tension was heavy in the air and things went from bad to worse. By Christmas, the church was in its greatest crisis in its history. There was no great feeling that God heard my prayers or honoured my fasting.

However, things eventually turned around. Could I say that the fast resulted in things getting better? Perhaps – I will never know. Others were praying too. But I do know that the fast did me no harm.

Fasting is a good thing to do if it is done without drawing attention to oneself and with sole regard to God's honour. However, not all people can fast, and those with medical conditions should consult their doctors before going on a fast. I never (not consciously anyway) made anybody feel guilty or less spiritual if they did not want to join in on a public fasting.

Fasting need not be limited to food. Dr Martyn Lloyd-Jones taught that fasting could be abstinence from anything that is legitimate – sleep, reading, good television, entertainment or whatever is very important to you, but which giving it up would be good for you at times.

When you fast, you should pray too – that is, if you possibly can. Some people have to work all day long when they are fasting, but be careful that you don't 'coast' on the knowledge that you are fasting, thinking that you don't need to read your Bible and pray. I would counsel you to exploit a time of fasting to the hilt; read the Bible all you can, pray all you can.

When should one fast? For one thing, if the burden is so great that you don't want food anyway, you might consider that this is an implicit call from God to fast for the moment. The psalmist said, 'My heart is blighted and withered like grass; I forget to eat my food' (Ps. 102:4). But undoubtedly the time when it is absolutely right to fast is when God hides his face for a long time: 'My tears have been my food day and night, while men say to me all day long, "Where is your God?"' (Ps. 42:3). As Isaiah put it, 'Truly you are a God who hides himself, O God and Saviour of Israel' (Isa. 45:15).

A time of crisis or emergency is an appropriate, perhaps even necessary, time to fast. When Mordecai challenged Esther to take a stand before the king, she asked 'all the

Jews who are in Susa' to 'fast for me' (Esther 4:16). It was a major turning point in the life of the Jews in that part of the world.

When you need direction from the Lord and clarification of what his will for you is, or when a major task is at hand, try fasting. If you are entering uncharted waters, try fasting. If there is a need for special power – or you are in the middle of persecution – try fasting. During a time of difficulty, 'Paul and Barnabas appointed elders for them in each church and, with prayer and fasting, committed them to the Lord, in whom they had put their trust' (Acts 14:23). If your church leadership calls for fasting, I urge you to submit to this.

I am not sure that regular, mechanical or liturgical fasting is a New Testament teaching. But if you feel led to do it, go for it! I have close friends who give up things for Lent every year. I did it once – I gave up mayonnaise. (I really hoped I would lose some weight – I didn't!) There is nothing wrong with giving up something for Lent as long as you don't think you are scoring points in heaven!

One of the greatest things a nation can do is to fast corporately, but this has not happened for many, many years. Great Britain did it during the Second World War. In my book *Thanking God*, I tell one of the most amazing stories in British history – how God stepped in and turned the war around as a result of a national day of prayer and fasting. We have this wonderful verse to recall: 'If my people, who are called by my name, will humble themselves and pray and seek my face and turn from their wicked ways, then will I hear from heaven and will forgive their sin and will heal their land' (2 Chron. 7:14). Fasting is not mentioned in this verse, but it would certainly be appropriate for people to fast when they claim this promise.

I have a ministerial friend who fasts whenever he is going to anoint someone with oil (according to James 5:14), to pray for healing. He does not do it to be seen by men; he feels the need for a greater faith and for power. I regard this as an admirable practice.

You can fast by missing one meal, two meals, or fast for a whole day, two days, or as many as you like (never more than forty though). My solemn advice, as I mentioned earlier, is to drink lots of water. You're not Moses – or Jesus. I have never gone on a forty-day fast – yet. I have no plans to do so either, but, who knows, maybe I will one day.

People also go on extended fasts for physical reasons. After a few days, some experience euphoria – entirely at the natural level. This is possibly because they get rid of a lot of toxins in the body. If you fast for spiritual reasons, and then after a few days experience this exhilarated feeling, be careful that you don't attribute it to the Holy Spirit; there is probably a natural explanation.

I repeat, the main thing is the honour of God. If you are fasting with the sole aim of seeking his face and not to gain personal glory, this can be a very good thing and I don't think you will regret it. I do believe you will see positive answers to your prayers – even if it is not immediate.

12

Faith and Feeling in Prayer

So Peter was kept in prison, but the church was earnestly praying to God for him. (Acts 12:5)

Do our feelings matter to God when we pray? Do they play a part in whether a prayer is answered?

I must now elaborate on a matter that I touched on in Chapter 2, and do so by posing a lot of questions.

Do you believe that the early Church's praying 'earnestly' for Peter was an essential ingredient as to whether God answered their prayer? Would one person offering a brief but sincere word of prayer on behalf of the Church have been equally effective – even if the Church had not continued in earnest praying? Does their earnestness indicate that they had *faith* or did it only mean they were praying non-stop?

These questions can be summed in one: are our prayers

more likely to be answered if we pray with feeling? I am not only addressing the issue of *faith* in praying, but also *feeling*. I suspect that you can have faith when you pray without much feeling; I equally suspect that you can have a lot of feeling without much faith! One could even make the case that at times the greater the feeling, the less faith there is. I think too it is possible for one's feelings to surface all the more simply because faith is *lacking*.

I am sure that the early Church's fervent praying for Peter in Acts 12 was accompanied with great feeling, deep concern, considerable anxiety and probably a lot of emotion. But I am not sure how much faith they actually had because when their prayer was suddenly answered, as we will see below, they didn't believe it!

What I want to know is, was their earnestness and fervency essential to their prayer? Did God himself take notice of this? Was there an inseparable connection between their persistency and the answered prayer? Does God look to see how deeply we feel before he answers?

I ask, then: do the words I say to God get answered by him whether they are perfunctorily uttered, or only when I pray with earnest feeling? And what if our faith is minimal?

During my time at Westminster Chapel I introduced a Prayer Covenant that included five petitions. Over three hundred people agreed to pray the five petitions each day. Not everybody was on board with the changes we made in the Chapel, hence the reason for the Prayer Covenant – to pray for unity. I did not ask or expect each person to pray the petitions day after day with agonising desperation. They merely repeated each petition to God – no doubt perfunctorily much of the time. I could not ask our people to intercede daily for years with the same depth of concern they would have, say, when they prayed for a loved one.

But it worked. It was not that every petition was answered (e.g. the one for true revival was not answered), but the general purpose of the Prayer Covenant was certainly fulfilled. It changed everything, and we had beautiful unity for many years.

The anxiety we feel when we pray will likely be in proportion to how close we are to the people for whom we pray. For example, I pray for Louise, T.R., Annette and Melissa with a greater concern and burden on my heart than I would for other people on my prayer lists. God himself affirms this. When Paul said, 'If anyone does not provide for his relatives, and especially for his immediate family, he has denied the faith and is worse than an unbeliever' (1 Tim. 5:8), it was an acknowledgement that we should have priorities in our relationships with people. We therefore are going to pray more carefully and persistently for those closest to us than we would for people outside our immediate family.

And yet when Paul said, 'Do not be anxious about anything' but 'present your requests to God' none the less (Phil. 4:6), one might argue that our prayers should *not* be immersed in desperation. A very high level of faith would almost certainly enable us to pray calmly and without being anxious. But how can any of us help but feel anxious when someone close to us is in great pain, is in a financial crisis, is desperately ill, or is waiting for the outcome of an important examination?

As for the early Church's praying for Peter, because of the situation at the time, I would not be surprised if they prayed for Peter as if he were a member of each person's own family. They were utterly gutted. They had not dreamed God would allow the wicked King Herod to arrest someone like James the brother of John – and put him to death. But he did. They could not imagine that Herod would arrest Simon Peter. But he did. Peter was now on Herod's hit list (Acts 12:1–4). This got the Church's attention and they prayed 'earnestly' for Peter ('without ceasing' – AV – Acts 12:5). The Greek word is *ektenes*. It means that deep and fervent prayer was offered for Peter in order that he be spared martyrdom. The Jerusalem Bible says that the Church prayed to God for him 'unremittingly'. The New English Bible uses the word 'fervently'.

I therefore ask: did this intensity of praying make a difference? Yes.

Did their strong feelings somewhat make up for their lack of faith? I believe so.

What we do know is that Peter was suddenly and miraculously delivered from prison and went straight to the place where the people were praying. When he turned up, they didn't believe it was Peter! And when they eventually did accept that it was him, they were still 'astonished' (Acts 12:6–16). This suggests to me that they had more *feeling* in their praying than they had faith! If so, God responded to their feeling more than he responded to their faith – which they seemed to have so little of.

I certainly do not underestimate the importance of faith when we pray. After all, if there is faith imparted by the Holy Spirit in our praying, the prayer will be answered. But what if there is little faith, but a lot of feeling? It seems to me that this is the best way to describe the people's fervent praying for Peter. And God stepped in. I am not saying they had no faith; I am saying they did not have a lot of faith.

It is my view that when our faith is minimal, God in his mercy sometimes honours our anxious feelings. He may take notice of our emotional involvement, our fears, our heart-felt burden – even if we do not have much faith.

There is a reason for this. It is not great faith that is required for God to step in; it is *any* degree of faith in a great God. We must focus on God, not our faith. We are all given a certain limit or 'measure' of faith (Rom. 12:3). The reason that our faith is limited is because none of us has the Holy Spirit without limit; only Jesus was given the Spirit without any limit (John 4:34). God therefore does not require a perfect faith in us; he asks us to persist and not give up. Indeed, Jesus taught that we should keep on praying and not give up (Luke 18:1). That very kind of persistence lay behind the early Church's praying for Peter.

This encourages me no end. I sometimes feel a little bit guilty that I do not have more faith. But when I get a glimpse of our compassionate *God* and how Jesus told us never, never, never to give up, I am given a burst of hope that keeps me asking God to answer my prayers.

Saving faith

This is a crucial issue when it comes to faith for salvation. There are several kinds of faith, and some of them may have nothing to do with salvation. For example, there is crisis faith – when you are in serious trouble and cry out to God in a crisis. There is temporal faith – when you periodically ask God to take care of your temporal needs. There is temporary faith – when you believe for a while, but not for very long.

But there is also *saving* faith – faith that assures us that we will go to heaven when we die. What makes faith *saving* faith? The issue is whether the *heart* was persuaded when the gospel was presented. This is why Paul said that we must not only confess with our mouths that Jesus is Lord, but believe in the 'heart' that Jesus was raised from the dead (Rom. 10:9–10). In other words, head-knowledge is not good enough. You may give mental assent to something, but is that saving faith? No, if it did not also find its way to the heart. The longest journey for all of us is from the head to the heart. Saving faith has emerged when the confession with your mouth is matched by belief in your heart.

It is not our great faith that achieves salvation; it is a measure of faith from the heart that trusts a great Saviour. That measure of faith is imparted by the Holy Spirit (2 Thess. 2:13).

The point is this. Heart-belief matters when it comes to becoming a Christian. You cannot be a true Christian if you do not believe the Bible in your *heart*, believe in your *heart* that Jesus was raised from the dead, and that his blood satisfies God's justice. You therefore profess your faith openly because you have been persuaded in your *heart*. A perfunctory confession of your faith – one that does not reach the heart – will be like a vaccination that doesn't 'take'.

Praying in faith

Heart-belief is essential to saving faith, but must the heart be equally engaged or persuaded when you pray regarding other things? How deeply must your heart be involved for your prayer to be heard when it comes to your prayer lists, or praying for healing, for revival, finances or other people's problems? After all, it was the *hearts* of the people that were engaged when they prayed for Peter.

Part of the answer is that one's heart will be engaged by *degrees*, according to the urgency of the request at the time. It depends on the situation and the people for whom we may be praying.

In this connection, there are possibly four kinds of praying that can result in answered prayer: (1) praying with great feeling and little faith; (2) praying with a higher level of faith but without much feeling; (3) praying with minimal faith and without much feeling; (4) praying with great feeling and great faith. I grant that my list could be extended, and that situations are not always so black or white.

But let us look at these premises a little more closely. Keep in mind that all four of these may result in God answering our prayers.

1 *Praying with great feeling, but little faith.* I would put the early Church's praying for the imprisoned Peter in Acts 12 in this category. Yes, there may have been varying degrees of faith among the believers as they prayed; some in the house possibly had more faith than others. But, generally speaking, they did not intercede with great faith but with an unwavering fervency.

And God stepped in. Are you surprised at this?

Why did God do it – when they seemed to have more anxiety about Peter than they had faith that God would answer them? I don't know. But you can be sure that God's greater concern for all of them – including Peter and his strategic role – was an essential factor. I do know that God honoured their fervent prayers. God had compassion on them. I also know that God would get all the glory! Nobody present could say, 'My faith did it!' There wasn't anybody who said, 'God told me Peter would be OK.'

They may have felt a bit ashamed that they had so little faith, especially when their prayer was answered right under their noses. Peter arrived at the place where they were praying and knocked on the door. A servant girl named Rhoda answered the door. She was so overjoyed that she ran back without opening it and exclaimed, 'Peter is at the door!' The instant, pessimistic reply from all those who had been praying for Peter was: 'You're out of your mind.' She pleaded with them to listen to her, but no: 'It must be his angel,' they argued. But when Peter kept on knocking and they finally opened the door and saw him, they were 'astonished' (Acts 12:13–16). Amazing.

I wonder if the reason God does not give us greater faith is because we might, just maybe, take ourselves a little bit too seriously if he answered all our prayers. But this is a prayer that God answered when more feeling than faith was in operation.

2 *Praying with a higher level of faith, but without much feeling*. This is when you may, or may not, have a warm feeling for the person. You may be emotionally detached in so far as being closely involved with this person or having great affection for them at a natural level. And yet you pray for them with an amazing assurance.

A good example of this is when you pray for your

enemies or those who have hurt you deeply. At the natural level you are upset; but your higher priority is the glory of God, and your esteem for the honour of God wins out.

This happened with Moses. He was angry with the people of Israel because they rebelled, and were unappreciative of him. God understood; he offered a 'deal' to Moses – to start all over again with a new nation. This meant destroying all the rebellious Israelites. Some people I know would have taken God's proposition with both hands! But not Moses. 'No,' he virtually said to God. 'I must turn down this proposition. You must forgive them. Your great name is at stake' (see Num. 14:11–16). God answered Moses' prayer (v. 20), and Moses knew that God would hear his intercession on behalf of Israel. He had a high level of faith that transcended his personal feelings about the Israelites. It was one of Moses' finest moments.

This can happen with you and me – we may be emotionally detached, but still pray with assurance. It does not have to involve an enemy or one who has hurt us. The point is: we are not emotionally involved and yet pray with a high level of faith. It may or may not happen when praying for a close friend or relative. It could of course – but it may more likely happen when the one who prays hardly knows the person he or she is praying for. It could happen when there was no opportunity to build a relationship with that person. It is faith with little or no feeling at work. Faith would make up for the absence of any feeling in this case.

If you were given a choice between faith or feeling, choose faith! It is better to have weak faith in a strong God than strong feeling. God sometimes honours our feeling, yes, as he did when the Church prayed for Peter. But he always honours the faith he imparted!

This does not mean that the person who prays in faith but without much feeling is devoid of compassion. It simply means that sometimes God imparts assurance of faith without there being a great measure of emotional involvement. For example, I know what it is to pray for someone I did not know and give a word of knowledge with little or no feeling. I have also known (at times) that what I have said was exactly right, but there was no engagement of my heart as I gave the word. This kind of praying usually comes when one is quite impartial, when one's ego is not a factor, or one is not too anxious to see results. But such a person is still an instrument of the Holy Spirit.

I have sometimes felt a little guilty that I had no feeling as I prayed or gave someone a word, especially when that person came back and thanked me profusely – as if I had done some great thing. The truth is that I sometimes would not even remember the occasion. I only know I can sometimes pray for a person with assurance of faith without much engagement of my heart, or give a word of assurance without any great sense of *compassion*. And yet sometimes God uses men and women who *least* need to see something extraordinary happen. A sympathetic detachment may mean that God will get the glory and we will be less tempted to draw attention to ourselves.

3 *Praying with minimal faith, and without much feeling.* It may surprise you that God answers prayers prayed in this manner, but he does. Eli was a priest in the place of worship at Shiloh. Whereas Hannah showed great emotion concerning being barren, Eli was annoyed with her, thinking she was drunk. When she convinced him otherwise, he perfunctorily gave her his blessing – with no display of great passion or faith: 'Go in peace, and may the God of Israel grant you what you have asked of him' (1 Sam. 1:17). I wonder if Eli ever expected to hear of her again. He obviously did not know who she was when she presented the boy Samuel to him later on (1 Sam. 1:24–28).

Neither Abraham nor Sarah showed great faith or excitement at the news that Sarah would conceive and bear a son. When Abraham first heard the news, he laughed and said to himself, 'Will a son be born to a man a hundred years old? Will Sarah bear a child at the age of ninety?' Not only that; Abraham was not even happy with the news; he asked God that Ishmael might be the promised child (Gen. 17:17–18). And when Sarah heard the news she too laughed and thought, 'After I am worn out and my master is old, will I now have this pleasure?' (Gen. 18:12)

Why would God use people whose faith is minimal and whose hearts are not always focused on what he wants? It is because God's greater strategy in his kingdom transcends our unworthiness.

Speaking personally, I have had the most unusual answers to prayer in this third category. Perhaps I should not have been, but I was *totally* surprised that God used our deacons and me in healing some people. For example, a deacon at Westminster Chapel and I anointed a lady with oil. This lady revealed an extraordinary story to us two years later. She had throat cancer. She came forward for prayer one evening by sitting where she would be prayed for by us. We do not remember praying for her and I am sure that I myself felt nothing when we prayed. In those days, people would sit on a pew and we would pray for each one briefly. In her case, three days later, after being prayed for, as she was being taken into the operating theatre in a London hospital – after one final X-ray – the operation was cancelled. The X-ray showed there was no cancer there at all. The lady, a very prominent Muslim, came to Christ as a result, was baptised, and became a member of the Chapel.

A lady from Chile asked us to pray for her husband. 'You healed me – now heal my husband,' she kindly commanded me. 'What? Healed you?' I asked. She replied, rather matter-of-factly, 'I had swollen leg for many years from snake bite in Chile. You prayed last Sunday. Monday morning – gone. My leg same size as other,' she said in broken English. 'No doctor, no medicine. Now heal my husband.'

Whoa! I could hardly take it in, but we proceeded to pray

for her husband whose problem was insomnia. 'I have not had a good night's sleep in twenty-five years,' he said to us. 'The spirits kick me out of bed.' We learned later that the man's mother was a witch in a coven. We anointed him with oil and prayed what I can only describe as a perfunctory prayer. I can't speak for the deacon with me, but for my part there was no feeling and certainly not a lot of faith. I felt nothing.

He returned the following Sunday. 'I slept three nights this week,' he said. 'Would you have another go?' We did, and the following Sunday he said he had slept every night 'like a baby'. Six months later, I invited him to give his testimony publicly.

In the summer of 2007, just after I gave an address at the CLAN (Christians Linked Across the Nation) conference in Scotland, a lady approached me and asked me to pray for her. 'I have a terrible sinus headache,' she told me. I then put my hands on her face and simply said, 'In Jesus' name be healed.' I had no assurance as I prayed and, although my heart to some extent went out to her, I was also in a hurry to keep an appointment. I would have forgotten this incident, but she wrote to me two months later and said, 'Do you remember praying for a lady when you were in St Andrews? I have had a sinus condition for five years. That day I had the worst headache of my entire life, I could hardly walk. When you prayed, I felt nothing. But four hours later I realised the pain was gone and it has never returned.'

What grips me is how God worked in wonderful ways even though I personally had minimal faith and compassion for these people. I have since prayed regularly for God to give me compassion for people when I pray for them, hoping of course this would result in more people being healed or delivered.

Praying with great feeling and great faith. This is what we aim for, and it describes how Jesus was all the time. He had perfect compassion and perfect faith, and no human being can match Jesus with such faith and compassion. What faith you and I have will be limited, and far, far short of Jesus' perfect faith.

Never forget that, as a man, Jesus had faith. 'I will put my trust in him' is a reference to Jesus' own faith (Heb. 2:13; Isa. 8:17). And yet Jesus' faith was the very faith of God. When Jesus said to the disciples, 'Have faith in God,' the Greek is *pistis theou* (literally, 'faith of God'). This is why he added:

> *I tell you the truth, if anyone says to this mountain, 'Go, throw yourself into the sea,' and does not doubt in his heart but believes that what he says will happen, it will be done for him. Therefore I tell you, whatever you ask for in prayer, believe that you have received it, and it will be yours.* (Mark 11:23–24)

This is an example of the faith of God. If God says to a

mountain, 'Throw yourself into the sea,' that mountain will disappear into the sea. God's faith is a perfect faith. When God said, 'Let there be light,' he did not doubt whether light would come; he believed it before it happened. And then, surprise, surprise, 'there was light' (Gen. 1:3).

If you and I really do believe we have received something before it has happened, it will be because the Holy Spirit imparted such a faith. You cannot 'work it up' or condition yourself to make it happen. It is what God does, and I don't think it happens every day.

But it happened to Jesus every day. The leper said to Jesus, 'Lord, if you are willing, you can make me clean.' Jesus replied, 'I am willing . . . Be clean!' (Matt. 8:3). A centurion begged Jesus to pray for his servant who was paralysed. Jesus simply said, 'I will go and heal him.' There was no wavering, no doubt, no agonising over whether this could happen. Jesus knew he would heal him. And he did – by 'remote control' as it happened; Jesus did not even need to be present to heal this man (Matt. 8:7–13). Jesus rebuked the storm on the lake – and it calmed down (Matt. 8:26). It is how he fed the multitudes with a little bit of bread and fish (Matt. 14:17–21); it is how he raised the dead (Luke 7:14; John 11:43–44). The reason? Jesus' faith. And yet his faith was the faith of God.

When people say that Jesus could not do some works because of the people's unbelief, I reply: Jesus could only do what the Father did. He said, 'I tell you the truth, the

Son can do nothing by himself; he can do only what he sees his Father doing, because whatever the Father does the Son also does' (John 5:19). Jesus could not heal many in Nazareth because the Father would not let him – as a rebuke to the people's rebellion, jealousy and rival spirit in his home town (Matt. 13:53–58). All that Jesus ever did – or didn't do – was out of perfect obedience to the Father. He trusted the Father with a perfect faith and did what he did for people with a perfect faith.

Not only that; his perfect faith was paralleled by perfect compassion. I am not sure which was more remarkable – Jesus' faith or his compassion. His compassion was extraordinary; here are some examples:

When he saw the crowds, he had compassion on them, because they were harassed and helpless, like sheep without a shepherd. (Matt. 9:36)

When Jesus landed and saw a large crowd, he had compassion on them and healed their sick. (Matt. 14:14)

I have compassion for these people; they have already been with me three days and have nothing to eat. I do not want to send them away hungry, or they may collapse on the way. (Matt. 15:32)

Jesus had compassion on them and touched their eyes.

Immediately they received their sight and followed him. (Matt. 20:34)

When the Lord saw her, his heart went out to her and he said, 'Don't cry.' (Luke 7:13)

It was perfect compassion and perfect faith in operation when Jesus walked on this planet, and behind the compassion of Jesus there is a compassionate, merciful God. This explains why the prayers of the early Church for Peter were answered despite the low level of faith among the people.

And yet God's mercy and compassion equally explain why he answers our prayers when we are short of compassion as well as faith. I quote it again: 'He knows how we are formed, he remembers that we are dust' (Ps. 103:14). He is not looking for strong faith; he is looking for people who trust in a strong God.

The anointing of oil

At Westminster Chapel we took seriously this passage in James:

Is any one of you sick? He should call the elders of the church to pray over him and anoint him with oil in the name of the Lord. And the prayer offered in faith will

make the sick person well; the Lord will raise him up.
If he has sinned, he will be forgiven. Therefore confess
your sins to each other and pray for each other so that
you may be healed. (James 5:14)

We invited people who wanted prayer for healing to come forward and to sit in the rows designated for this. This would be their way of calling for the 'elders of the church'. The deacons functioned as elders during this time, with two or more of them always praying for the person requesting prayer. Why two? So if there was a healing, nobody knew for sure which deacon prayed the prayer of faith!

Why oil? You tell me. We simply followed the Scripture literally.

The Authorised Version refers to the 'prayer of faith', a more literal translation from the Greek, as opposed to the New International Version translation of 'the prayer offered in faith'. We are certainly talking about a prayer offered in faith, but I have long suspected that the prayer of faith may not be consciously felt by the one doing the praying. What if it is the prayer of Jesus behind the scene that is in operation? For example, in no case when I myself have prayed for people with anointing oil have I felt my prayer was anything but ordinary. In other words, I felt no conscious witness of the Spirit that someone would be healed. But the examples I give above indicated that some people *were* healed.

It is my view that the faith of Jesus at the right hand of

God overruled our lack of faith and compassion on these occasions. We prayed as best as we could and as earnestly as we knew how, but we never knew if a person would be healed. This is why I believe that the faith of Christ overruled at times. He did it all; we were only willing instruments.

If you want more information on his, I would point you to my expositions on James in which I go into more detail (*Justification by Works, The Way of Wisdom*, 2 vols, Christian Focus).

Since living in America I have had the privilege of spending a little time with Oral Roberts. He told me he would *feel* the anointing for healing (usually in his right hand) when he prayed for people. He did not apparently use oil. I have no doubt that thousands were healed through his ministry, and I believe his anointing was unique. I would love to have such anointing! In the meantime, I shall pray for more compassion and more faith as I continue to pray for people's healing before I go to heaven.

Try tears

The issue in this chapter is this: how important are faith and feeling when we pray? My conclusion is: if faith seems absent, try tears. I cannot prove it, but I would guarantee that the people praying for Peter in Acts 12 shed tears.

The first time the word 'tears' is mentioned in the Bible

is when Hezekiah was told he would die. When a prophet like Isaiah tells you that, you take it seriously. Hezekiah did, but it didn't stop him from praying. He pleaded with the Lord and 'wept bitterly'. God stepped in. He told Isaiah to go back to Hezekiah with a very wonderful word: 'I have heard your prayer and *seen your tears*; I will heal you' (emphasis mine, 2 Kgs. 20:5). If the 'law of first mention' is to be taken seriously (as some scholars believe), this account tells us that tears get God's attention.

Are you desperate? God can use your tears. Do you want to be healed? God can use your tears. Are you in extreme difficulty? God can use your tears. 'He who goes out weeping, carrying seed to sow, will return with songs of joy, carrying sheaves with him' (Ps. 126:6). Try tears.

In one of David's darkest hours – when in exile after being betrayed by Absalom – he received news that his friend and confidant Ahithophel had also turned against him. He also knew that Ahithophel gave such a word of wisdom that it was seen as tantamount to being the voice of God (2 Sam. 16:23). David wept as he continued up the Mount of Olives, having heard of Ahithophel's joining Absalom. He simply prayed: 'O LORD, turn Ahithophel's counsel into foolishness' (2 Sam. 15:31). I don't know how much faith David exercised in that awful hour, I only know he wept as he prayed. God miraculously stepped in and answered David's prayer: 'For the LORD had determined to frustrate the good advice of Ahithophel in order to bring disaster on Absalom' (2 Sam. 17:14).

In Chapter 4 I made mention of one of my heroes, Robert Murray M'Cheyne. In the summer of 2007 I was invited to speak in Robert Murray M'Cheyne's old pulpit in Dundee, Scotland. It was a peak experience for me, I will never forget it. I have stood in awe of M'Cheyne for over fifty years. M'Cheyne saw true revival in his church, but died at the age of twenty-nine. Six months later a young minister visited the church and sought out one of the elders, and asked what a person could do to have M'Cheyne's success. 'Oh, I can tell you,' said the wise elder. 'Come with me. Sit here at M'Cheyne's desk. Now put your elbows on the desk and put your face in your hands. And let the tears flow. Now come with me. Stand here in his pulpit. Put your elbows on the pulpit and put your face in your hands. And let the tears flow.'

It is no doubt the case that some people can 'work up' tears, and I am certainly not talking about phoney tears here. But when they flow from a distraught and desperate heart, I believe they touch God. In some way that I will not try to explain or justify, I believe that a broken and contrite heart is a definite way to make up for our lack of faith. That is why God answers the prayers of some who admit their faith is so weak.

So if compassion and feeling are there, but you feel lacking in faith, it can still be worthwhile.

Jesus' compassion mirrors God's compassion, and this is why God is touched by our feelings of desperation. If our faith is minimal, the compassion and heart-felt concern we feel might – just maybe – make up for the lack of faith. Therefore when we feel deeply and long for God to step in, but are so limited in faith, remember that God sometimes honours our deepest feelings after all. He reveals his compassion by stepping in, by deliverances, by healing people, by miraculous answers to prayer. Yes, even if there is not a lot of faith. A lack of faith is not necessarily rebellious unbelief; it may be our longing for God to work without our having the faith we wish we had. God does not rebuke those who say, 'I do believe; help me overcome my unbelief!' (Mark 9:24). God knows how we are formed; he remembers we are dust. When the disciples said to Jesus, 'Increase our faith!' (Luke 17:5), he did not make them feel guilty about not having great faith. Instead, he encouraged them regarding what could be achieved with just a small amount of faith.

We cannot be perfectly like Jesus. Only Jesus had a perfect faith and perfect compassion.

So I take encouragement from knowing that my feelings matter. I am simply not able to produce faith. Or compassion. But when I am hurting, sad, broken and worried – whether regarding my family, close friends, God's church all over the world, or my own personal concerns – I try to remember always that God may be attracted to our sorrowful feelings. 'The LORD is close to the broken-hearted and saves those who are crushed in spirit' (Ps. 34:18).

Standing somewhere in the shadows you'll find Jesus;
He's the only one who cares and understands;
Standing somewhere in the shadows you'll find Jesus;
And you'll know him by the nail prints in his hands.
(Anon.)

No matter what may bring it about, a broken and contrite heart is a heart that God will never despise (Ps. 51:17). As Bernard of Clairvaux (1091–1153) put it, Jesus is the 'hope of every contrite heart'.

13

Praying in the Spirit

Pray in the Holy Spirit. (Jude 20)

Praying in the Spirit is praying in the will of God, and there is no higher level of praying than this. No word uttered in our praying, no prayer request, no petition or any desire of ours could surpass the timing or wisdom of the will of God. Effectual praying and the will of God are inseparable in the kind of praying God wants for you and me. If you want your prayers to be answered, then pray in the will of God. You will never – ever – do better than God's will in any case, but the person who tries to bypass God's will in praying is a fool.

Praying in the Spirit guarantees that you will pray in the will of God.

God only wants what is best for us, and his will is superior to anything you and I would have come up wi

He has carefully designed your life and mine as if there were no other lives in the universe. Trust him to have worked it out already; don't try to improve on his plan.

We are therefore commanded to pray in the Spirit because that is the way to be sure you are praying in the will of God. And we are commanded to pray in the Spirit in at least two places – Ephesians 6:18 and Jude 20 – and Paul refers to praying in the Spirit in Romans 8:26–27, to which I will return below.

Although praying in the Spirit is praying in the will of God, we do not always *know* we are actually praying in the will of God. The only way we can be heard by God is to pray in his will, but praying in his will and actually *knowing* we are doing it are sometimes two different things. This is why John says, '*If* we ask anything according to his will, he hears us' (emphasis mine, 1 John 5:14). This is a big 'if'. If only we all did it! And yet we are commanded to. It is much the same thing as knowing what the will of the Lord is. Paul says, 'Do not be foolish, but understand what the Lord's will is' (Eph. 5:17). If only we always did!

When John talks about God 'hearing' us, he speaks as a Hebrew; it is Hebraic-type thinking. It goes back to the Hebrew word *shamar* – to hear. Every ancient Jew knew the 'Shemah': 'Hear, O Israel: The LORD our God, the LORD is one' (Deut. 6:4). And yet the Hebrew word not only means to hear but also 'to obey'. A parent will sometimes say to their child '*Did you hear me?*' if he or she is not obeying. In Hebrew, to hear was also to obey.

Therefore when God 'hears' us, it means he also obeys our request. That is the meaning of Isaiah's words, 'You cannot fast as you do today and expect your voice to be *heard* on high' (emphasis mine, Isa. 58:4). In order to be heard by God, we must pray in his will. Praying in the Spirit, then, is praying in God's will. Let me put two scenarios to you:

Scenario One: you pray with amazing *understanding*

Do you know what it is to have a clear sense of thinking as you pray, aware that you are praying in the will of God? I have known it on occasions, but it certainly does not happen to me every day. It is a conscious intercession whereby you feel the enabling of the Holy Spirit in what you *say* to God and put through to the throne of grace. You can sense you are being 'heard'. John stated that answered prayer is only promised if we pray in God's will. He also put the possibility of knowing that you have been heard. This is why John throws in yet another 'if': 'If we *know that he hears us* – whatever we ask – we know that we have what we asked of him' (emphasis mine, 1 John 5:15). Have you experienced this? How often?

This is praying in the Holy Spirit.

Some rather 'pious' person may say, 'If you were as spiritual as you should be, you would always know that you pray in the will of God.' Really? What about the Apostle Paul? Would you consider him a spiritual person?

And yet in Romans 8:26–27 he claims he does not always know how to pray or what to say!

Scenario Two: you pray with minimal *understanding*

Do you also know what it is to want to pray, but you don't know what to say? Have you had times when the burden was so great that you only wanted to groan and could not utter an intelligible phrase in your prayer? Have you sensed the intercession of the Spirit, but you have no idea what the Spirit was actually saying? Have you wished you could know what he is actually putting to God on your behalf? Have you experienced the Spirit's intercession 'with groans that words cannot express' (Rom. 8:26)? Have you had occasion to pray, but 'words failed'?

This too is praying in the Holy Spirit.

It is a great thing if *either* of these scenarios *ever* describes you when you pray.

In Scenario One, the Holy Spirit has allowed you 'in' on the content (or at least part of it) of his intercession, and he is a far better intercessor than you and I will ever be. When you pray with this kind of authority, as the disciples prayed in Acts 4:24–30 (which we saw above), you can be sure that the intercession on your behalf is in accordance with the will of God. It is part of the Spirit's 'job description' to assist you in your praying, and when there is an authoritative anointing such as this, it is praying in the Spirit.

In Scenario Two, the Holy Spirit intercedes secretly on your behalf, not communicating to you what he is actually praying. You are therefore not allowed 'in' on the content of his intercession. It is described by Paul in these lines:

The Spirit helps us in our weakness. We do not know what we ought to pray for, but the Spirit himself intercedes for us with groans that words cannot express. And he who searches our hearts knows the mind of the Spirit, because the Spirit intercedes for the saints in accordance with God's will. (Rom. 8:26–27)

The Spirit's intercession is effectual – his prayer will be answered, but you are not allowed to know what the secret will of God is. The joy in experiencing Scenario Two is in knowing that the Holy Spirit is interceding on your behalf according to what is his will for you. Never forget that God only wants what is best for us, and we should be content to know we are in good hands. Of course we would like to know what he is actually praying, but this is why it is secret – for now.

Both scenarios, then, are examples of praying in the Spirit.

The truth is that we actually have two persons of the Godhead who intercede for us all the time:

First, our Great High Priest, the person of the Lord Jesus

189

Christ, prays for us. He is at God's right hand, always interceding for those who come to God by him (Heb. 7:25). As we have seen already, he is touched by the feeling of our 'weaknesses' (Greek: *astheneia* – Heb. 4:15). This is wonderful news. Jesus is right now at God's right hand 'interceding for us' (Rom. 8:34).

Second, we have the person of the Holy Spirit interceding for us. The Holy Spirit indwells each of us, but also prays for us. He too helps us in our 'weakness' (same Greek word, *astheneia*). The Spirit not only convicted us of our sin (John 16:7–8), but effectually drew us to the Father (John 6:44) when we were converted. But that is not all; he even intercedes for us.

The intercessory prayers of the Son and the Spirit have this in common: they are offered to the Father with a perfect faith and in perfect accordance with the will of God. Jesus never puts an ill-posed request to the Father on our behalf. He only asks for that which is the Father's will. After all, a prerequisite for answered prayer is to pray in God's will. Never forget this. 'If we ask anything according to his will, he hears us' (1 John 5:14). The same is true of the Holy Spirit. The Holy Spirit intercedes for us according to God's will (Rom. 8:27). In a word: the Son and the Spirit will never pray out of the will of God, only in the will of God for us.

You and I are invited, indeed commanded, to pray 'in the Spirit'. If we truly do this, we can be sure – absolutely sure – that two things will follow: (1) we pray in the will of

God, and (2) what the Spirit prays for us will be answered. If we pray in the flesh, thankfully our prayer will not be answered. God politely and lovingly ignores foolish requests unless we persist in what is against God's will for us. Never forget that ominous word: 'He gave them what they asked for, but sent a wasting disease upon them' (Ps. 106:15). Ancient Israel demanded a king, and they got what they wanted. They pursued this because they were in unbelief; they rejected God's revealed will (1 Sam. 8:6–9). The prophet Hosea later said: 'So in my anger I gave you a king, and in my wrath I took him away' (Hos. 13:11).

The most important thing about prayer is the will of God.

Never – ever – try to upstage God's will. I will say it again: if you want to be a complete fool, try to do better than God's will for your life.

The most wonderful thing about the Holy Spirit's intercession for us is that he prays in accordance with God's will. All that we can do of value must be done through the help of the Holy Spirit. Jesus said, 'The Spirit gives life; the flesh counts for nothing' (John 6:63). We are to live by the Spirit (Gal. 5:16). Paul preached with a demonstration of the Spirit's power (1 Cor. 2:4; 1 Thess. 1:5). Stephen spoke by the Spirit (Acts 6:10). Disciples prophesied through the Spirit (Acts 21:4). Truth is revealed by the Spirit (John 14:26; 1 Cor. 2:14). The early Church ministered by the Spirit (Gal. 3:5). We wait by the Spirit (Gal. 5:5). We walk by the Spirit (Gal. 5:25). We live by the testimony of the Spirit (1 John 5:6). We worship by the Spirit (Phil. 3:3). We are sealed by the Spirit (Eph. 1:13). We have the earnest of the Spirit (2 Cor. 1:22). We are led by the Spirit (Rom. 8:14).

It therefore should not surprise us that we are commanded to *pray* in the Spirit. Paul ended his letter to the Ephesians: 'And *pray in the Spirit* on all occasions with all kinds of prayers and requests' (emphasis mine, Eph. 6:18). Jude exhorted: 'But you, dear friends, build yourselves up in your most holy faith and *pray in the Holy Spirit*' (emphasis mine, Jude 20).

Why would Paul and Jude exhort us to pray in the Spirit? What good does it do? First, it ensures we pray in the will of God. But, second, it is effectual in spiritual warfare – when we are conscious of the enemy's opposition. Paul's reference to praying in the Holy Spirit was in the context of the greatest passage in the New Testament on spiritual warfare. In a paragraph that began with the words, 'Be strong in the Lord and in his mighty power', leading to that striking comment, 'For our struggle is not against flesh and blood, but against the rulers, against the authorities, against the powers of this dark world' (Eph. 6:10, 12), Paul actually ends with, 'And pray in the Spirit on all occasions with all kinds of prayers and requests' (Eph. 6:18). Having told us to know what God's will is (Eph. 5:17), he now commands us to pray within it. It is the prayer that effectively defeats the work of Satan.

Jude gave the command to pray in the Holy Spirit in a

letter that warned the Church against opposition to the gospel. The earliest theological threat to the early Church was Gnosticism (from the Greek *gnosis* – knowledge), where a novel way of 'knowing' was brought into the Church. It was a lot like New Age thinking today. Wherever it penetrated the Church, the gospel was undermined. Warning against certain men who brought in their heresies and sensual way of life, Jude exhorted the Church to build themselves up in their most holy faith and pray in the Holy Spirit (v. 20). The situation was too desperate to pray any other way.

Praying in the Spirit, then, is carried out in two ways: (1) praying consciously in the will of God, and (2) groaning in prayer because you don't know what the specific will of God in every situation is.

Are these two premises contradictory? No. The first refers to God's revealed will (the Bible); the second refers to his secret will that will remain secret – at least for the moment. When you pray according to the revealed will of God – what is unveiled in Scripture – you know your praying is absolutely right, because the will of God will always be in accordance with his *Word*. This is when you put things to God that would never be contradictory to what he has revealed in his Word – the Bible. But when you pray according to the secret will of God, which the Holy Spirit knows perfectly, you acquiesce to *his* wisdom – not yours.

Praying consciously in the will of God

This is done by the aid of the Holy Spirit; you cannot do this in the flesh. The flesh is not capable of letting you pray in the Holy Spirit. First, the flesh wants the opposite of the Spirit (Gal. 5:17). Second, the flesh has no way of knowing the will of God.

However, as I mentioned briefly in Chapter 4, the Puritans believed that the will of God is basically grasped in two ways: (1) the revealed will of God (Scripture), and (2) the secret will of God (the future). We now return to this very important matter.

People often ask, 'How can I know the will of God?' They usually pose this question with a view to knowing what they should do with their lives, what kind of jobs they should take, whether they are called to preach, to marry a particular person, where to go on holiday, which church to go to, what God wants them to do next, etc.

The revealed will of God is the Bible, and the best way to know the will of God is to know the Bible, God's own Word. When Ananias said to Saul of Tarsus, 'The God of our fathers has chosen you to know his will' (Acts 22:14), it was primarily referring to an ability to understand Scripture.

But most people do not want to know the will of God earnestly and eagerly enough simply to seek his will by reading his Word. They may say that it takes too long. As we saw earlier, people nowadays seem to want a *rhema* Word – an immediate, direct word from the Most High.

This appeals to all of us, especially if we are busy people – always in a hurry.

The truth is that those who care enough to read their Bibles daily – and keep it up – are those who are more likely to know what his will is. This is true even with regard to the kind of matters I just raised above vis-à-vis those merely eager for a 'quick word'. It is the long-term relationship with God and his Word that pays incalculable dividends when it comes to knowing what his will is.

To summarise: there are two kinds of praying in the Spirit: *knowing* what God's will is (1 John 5:15) and *not knowing* what God's will is (Rom. 8:26–27).

Praying without bitterness

The question follows: *how* do we pray in the Holy Spirit? The answer? It is praying without bitterness. You pray in the Spirit by putting your requests to God from a heart devoid of bitterness. You cannot truly pray in the Spirit when the Spirit is grieved. Paul warned us: 'Do not grieve the Holy Spirit of God' (Eph. 4:30). The Greek word that is translated 'grieve' means hurt feelings. The Holy Spirit is a person with feelings, and he gets his feelings hurt when we are angry, bitter and unforgiving. Grieving the Spirit does not result in you losing your salvation, but you do forfeit the sense of his presence and a certain ability to pray in the revealed will of God. You will be playing games with yourself if you claim you are praying in the Spirit and holding a grudge against someone at the same time. The most important thing, then, is praying in line with the revealed will of God with no bitterness.

Therefore as long as the Holy Spirit is in you *ungrieved* – which means he is at home with you – you will be praying in the Spirit by pouring your heart out to God according to the need at hand. Remember the principles I have sought to teach in this book, then put your requests to God with all your heart. You may find yourself in Scenario One, when you sense that what you are asking will be given to you; or you may find yourself in Scenario Two, when you have no understanding of what God's will is as you pray.

I now must stress this point, because it is one of the most important issues in this book. *The key to praying in the Spirit is learning to pray without any bitterness in our hearts.* It means manifesting the fruits of the Spirit – 'love, joy, peace, patience, kindness, goodness, faithfulness, gentleness and self-control' (Gal. 5:22–23). This equally means learning *not* to grieve the Holy Spirit, and the chief way we tend to do this is by being bitter. Paul knew this and gave this command: 'Get rid of all bitterness, rage and anger, brawling and slander, along with every form of malice. Be kind and compassionate to one another, forgiving each other, just as in Christ God forgave you' (Eph. 4:30–32).

Not grieving the Spirit and manifesting the fruits of the Spirit come to the same thing. The fruits of the Spirit will flow in us to the degree we do not grieve the Spirit by bitterness, anger and unforgiveness.

I'm sorry, but I cannot promise you that there will ever be praying in the Spirit if you are holding a grudge and refusing to forgive. You cannot say, 'I think I will try praying in the Spirit for a while in order to get my prayers answered', and expect to do this when you have not been living in total forgiveness. Total forgiveness and praying in the Spirit are as important to each other as breathing and living are to each other. You will recall that the passage concerning prayer that moves mountains was immediately followed by Jesus' words, 'And when you stand praying, if you hold anything against anyone, forgive him.' Jesus said, 'Whatever you ask for in prayer, believe that you have received it, and it will be yours' (Mark 11:23–25), and he repeated this principle in 1 John 5:15: 'And if we know that he hears us – whatever we ask – we know that we have what we asked of him.'

In a word: totally forgiving those who have hurt or maligned us is a prerequisite to knowing that you are praying in the will of God. It is therefore crucial to forgive all who have hurt you if you want to pray in the Spirit.

But it is also very important to know God's Word if you expect to pray according to his revealed will – the Bible.

Those who know their Bibles are more likely to pray consciously with the knowledge of God's will. For example, they will already know *not* to ask for certain things. They would not ask God to do anything that goes against the Ten Commandments – or Jesus' interpretation of them in

Matthew 5. For example, you would never ask God to do anything for you that is sinful. He will not lead you to do what he has already outlawed. You will not be granted to kill people, steal or engage in sex outside marriage. According to Jesus, you are also prohibited to hate, carry grudges, or have lust in your heart. In other words, those who pray in the will of God will only ask for that which is consistent with all that is written in the New Testament. Here is an important verse in this connection: 'My people are destroyed from lack of knowledge' (Hos. 4:6).

When John said we must ask according to God's will in order to be heard, he means that we must ask in accordance to his *Word*. Below is an acrostic that I have shared with many people around the world to help them know the will of God. If you are wanting to do something, to feel 'led' to do this or that – or are praying about a matter and you want to be sure you are proceeding in God's will – ask:

P – is it *providential?* Does the door open without you knocking it down?
E – what do you suppose your *enemy* (the devil) would want? Do the opposite.
A – what is your *authority* (the Bible) for continuing? Is it biblical?
C – does your *confidence* increase or diminish at the thought of this?
E – do you have *ease* in your heart of hearts at the thought of this?

In short, make sure you do the things that make for peace (Rom. 14:19). You need *five out of five* of the above propositions for this acrostic to work for you. One out of five, even four out of five, won't do. But if it is providential, if you have a pretty shrewd idea what the devil would want (and make sure you do the opposite), if it is clearly not against Scripture but in accordance with it, if your confidence increases and you have inner ease, you are probably on safe ground. Shakespeare put it well: 'To thine own self be true.'

When you live by the principles such as I have outlined above, you are almost certainly going to pray in the will of God. Praying according to the revealed will of God is what I mean by Scenario One at the beginning of this chapter. It presupposes that you know your Bible fairly well and that you live in total forgiveness.

God's secret will refers to things hidden from us – for example, the future. We are all fascinated by the possibility of knowing what the future holds, but unless the Holy Spirit *shows* us the future, we cannot possibly know it. Keep in mind the following: God knows the future, perfectly. He knows the future as totally as he knows the past. If he wants to, he can show you what lies ahead for you.

It is not every day that one can pray consciously in the will of God regarding what he will do in the future. Unless God prophetically puts things before you (which he can do if he wills it), you will only be speculating when it comes to this matter. Stay away from it; don't try to figure it out.

However, this is where praying with groaning in the Spirit comes in because the Holy Spirit within you can intercede for you. You may *wish* he would tell you what he is praying, but he probably won't. That is why you pray with groaning and not with clear knowledge. The prayer is absolutely effectual because it is the Spirit interceding, not you, and the Holy Spirit only prays in accordance with the will of God.

The Authorised Version puts it like this: the Spirit intercedes 'with groanings which cannot be uttered'. Today's English Version states: 'in groans that words cannot express'. The New English Bible: 'through our inarticulate groans the Spirit himself is pleading for us'. The Revised Standard Version: 'the Spirit himself intercedes for us with sighs too deep for words'. Phillips Modern English: 'his Spirit within us is actually praying for us in those agonizing longings which cannot find words'.

The Holy Spirit, in not telling us what he is praying, does this intercession in accordance with the will of God. We don't know what he is asking for, but we know this much: his prayer for us is exactly right! It is in God's will. That is good enough for me.

Could Romans 8:26–27 refer to *praying in tongues*? Yes, providing that one simultaneously manifests the fruits of the Spirit – namely, total forgiveness. Therefore praying in tongues that flows from the ungrieved Spirit in us is at least part of the explanation to this unusual passage. One does not have to pray in tongues to pray in the Spirit, but praying in tongues – when flowing also out of the *fruits* of the Spirit – certainly *is* praying in the Spirit.

Therefore when Paul and Jude exhort us to pray in the Spirit, do they mean praying in tongues? Almost certainly. And yet one can groan in his or her spirit, according to Romans 8:26–27, and not pray in tongues. It would be a mistake to say you cannot pray in the Spirit if you do not pray in tongues. After all, praying consciously in the will of God is not praying in tongues; it is consciously knowing you are asking for things that honour and glorify God. Therefore you can also groan in your spirit and not pray in tongues.

However, it is my view that those who do pray in tongues have an 'edification advantage' over those who do not. I do not mean they are better Christians or more spiritual, but I do believe that they enjoy a greater measure of edification and blessing than those who do not pray in tongues. Paul said that anyone who 'speaks in a tongue does not speak to men but to God' (1 Cor. 14:2) which shows they are praying. Paul states that (1) the person is speaking to *God*, (2) what the person says is unintelligible ('no one understands him; he utters mysteries with his spirit'), (3) he or she is edified – built up (1 Cor. 14:2).

Let me address a matter that may be a little bit controversial. The evangelical sector of the Church today is loosely divided between those who are non-charismatic and those who are charismatic. The word 'charismatic' comes from the Greek word *charisma*, which simply means 'grace-gift'. Put simplistically, charismatic Christians believe in and experience the gifts of the Spirit; non-charismatic Christians don't – although many would say they believe in all the gifts except tongues.

One difference between these two camps, according to my own observation, is that non-charismatic Christians stress the *fruits* of the Spirit – 'love, joy, peace, patience, kindness, goodness, faithfulness, gentleness and self-control' (Gal. 5:22–23). Charismatic Christians, while certainly believing in the fruits of the Spirit, tend to emphasise the *gifts* of the Spirit – wisdom, the word of knowledge, faith, healing, miracles, prophecy, discernment of spirits, speaking in tongues and interpretation of tongues (1 Cor. 12:8–10). I would further observe that, generally speaking, non-charismatic Christians eagerly embrace *all* the gifts of the Spirit – other than tongues.

My friend Charles Carrin has made the interesting observation that the gift of tongues is the only gift of the Spirit that challenges your *pride*, and I'm afraid he may be right. There is no stigma with the gifts of wisdom, knowledge, prophecy or healing. But there *is* a stigma with *tongues*.

This chapter is not intended to persuade you to pray in tongues – though if I thought I could succeed, I would try – because I would be doing you a great favour. My motive is simply to be a good expositor of Scripture and tell you what praying in the Spirit is. It partly refers to praying in tongues, and I would ask you on bended knee not to dismiss it out of hand.

It is a wonderful satisfaction to pray in tongues when claiming Romans 8:26–27. Do read these verses again. They make the most sense when you put praying in tongues into the equation. The best thing of all, however, is that when I pray in tongues it is *one time I know for sure I am praying in the will of God* – regarding his *secret* will!

When you pray in tongues, you put your desires in neutral – for the moment. When you pray in tongues, you cannot dictate to the Father, the Son and the Spirit what you want. You are out of the picture – except for praying in the Spirit. Once you begin praying in tongues, you acquiesce to the sovereign will of God. I know people who will pray in tongues for someone – or a particular situation. I can understand them doing this, but the truth is that while you are praying in tongues you take your hands off the 'control button'. Praying in tongues does not add substance to your prayer; it is letting God be God. It is perfectly right to pray in tongues when you are burdened for someone or something, but keep in mind that the Holy Spirit will only intercede according to God's will – not yours.

When I pray in tongues, I am saying, 'Your will be done, Lord.' I am not trying to twist God's arm to do things my way. When I pray in tongues I am submitting to *his* way.

This is very important. We must not make the mistake of thinking that our praying in tongues is going to change

God's mind. Praying in tongues is *submitting* to God's will. And when you add other spiritual requests, whatever they are or however great they may be, you submit to God's wisdom.

To put it another way: when you pray in the Spirit you do not change God's mind but *you* are changed. It edifies, it builds you up; it makes you stronger; it gives you more grace to resist the enemy.

No, I don't know what I am saying when I pray in tongues. Furthermore, the devil does not know what I am saying either! A friend of mine used to say, 'It is the only time the devil doesn't know what you are saying!' But, yes, *God* knows! This is because the same God who knows us backwards and forwards, and knows the future perfectly, also 'knows the mind of the Spirit, because the Spirit intercedes for the saints in accordance with God's will' (Rom. 8:27). And no, the Holy Spirit will not tell me what he is praying – whether I am praying in tongues or merely praying with 'sighs' that words cannot express.

But I am content that his praying is perfect – and I can leave it at that.

Can you? Are you willing not to know?

One final caution: praying in tongues is not a sure sign of spirituality. That is one of the biggest differences between the *gifts* of the Spirit and the *fruits* of the Spirit. The gifts of the Spirit do not prove spirituality; the fruits do. This is because the gifts of the Spirit are without repentance – irrevocable (Rom. 11:29). If King Saul – a backslider if ever there was one – could prophesy when he was trying to kill David (1 Sam. 19:23–24), it is not surprising that people could maintain other gifts of the Spirit and live unacceptable lives. Therefore do not think that praying in tongues means you are necessarily where you ought to be in your walk with the Lord!

The way to be sure that you are walking in the Spirit is not through the exercise of the gifts, but by the fruits of the Spirit. When the fruits of the Spirit mean as much to you as the gifts – and you manifest both – you are reflecting what will bring honour to God and keep your life from being a disgrace to his name.

Praying in the Spirit is edifying. It is a threat to the devil. It is pleasing to God. So whether you are praying consciously in the will of God – or praying with groans (or tongues) without knowing what his will is – you are being true to God. And when you are true to God, you are true to yourself.

PART FIVE

The Mystery of Prayer

14

Answered Prayer

*Do not be afraid, Zechariah; your prayer has
been heard.* (Luke 1:13)

Although the greatest fringe benefit of being a Christian
is the privilege of prayer, the subject of prayer remains
one of the greatest theological mysteries of all.

There are mainly two difficult questions I want to raise.
In the present chapter I ask, why does God invite us to pray
when he already knows everything *and* has promised
already to withhold nothing good from us? In our final
chapter I will ask, why does he, being a God of integrity
who cannot lie, promise to answer prayer – but does not
(apparently) always keep his promise?

Why, then, do we pray? Answer: we want God to hear us.
We pray because we want God to step in and act on our
behalf. As I said earlier, prayer can be generally defined as

asking God to act, and when he does act it is an event most wonderful indeed. To experience answered prayer brings about one of the greatest joys there is. 'In my distress I called to the LORD, and he answered me,' said Jonah (Jonah 2:2). 'They called on the LORD and he answered them' (Ps. 99:6). 'When I called, you answered me' (Ps. 138:3).

God motivates us to pray largely by his promise to answer our prayer. 'He will call upon me, and I will answer him' (Ps. 91:15). 'Call to me and I will answer you and tell you great and unsearchable things you do not know' (Jer. 33:3). Jesus gave a parable 'to show them that they should always pray and not give up' (Luke 18:1). Peter quoted Psalm 34:15: 'The eyes of the Lord are on the righteous and his ears are attentive to their prayer' (1 Pet. 3:12).

I want to relate an account of a beautiful answer to prayer which I heard the Revd Robert Morris, pastor of Gateway Church in South Lake, Texas, give on James Robison's TV show. Robert tells of a man who had a prayer list of unsaved people he prayed for to become Christians. He put the names of the people he witnessed to in the back of his Bible and would pray for them until they were saved. Here is Robert Morris's story:

My grandfather used to work for the Texas Highway Department with a guy called Ray Alexander – a believer. Their job was to put asphalt in potholes. Ray witnessed to my grandfather and said, 'Why don't you come over tonight after dinner and let me share more

*with you about Jesus?' So my grandfather said, 'OK.'
After dinner he got up and started to leave, and my
father – then aged sixteen – said to him, 'Where are
you going?' My grandfather said, 'I'm going to talk to
a man.' My father had just gotten his driver's license
and asked, 'Can I drive you?' My grandfather said,
'Yes, but you have to stay outside while we talk.'*

*So they drove over; my father sat alone in the car.
Finally he became a little bored, so he got out of the
car, and he went up and sat on the steps of the front
porch. There was no air conditioning back then, so the
door was open. For the first time, my father heard the
gospel – that Jesus was the Son of God, came to the
earth and died on the cross for our sins. Ray
Alexander said to my grandfather, 'Would you like to
accept Jesus as your Saviour?' My grandfather said,
'No, I want to think about it.' Ray then said to my
grandfather, 'Then, if you ever decide to get saved,
pray a prayer like this.' And as he went through the
sinner's prayer, my father, sitting on the front porch,
actually prayed that prayer and got saved. He raised
me in a Christian home, and I too became a Christian,
then became an evangelist, did stadium crusades,
preached in churches – and saw thousands of people
saved. Now, through Gateway Church, we've seen
thousands more saved.*

*A few years before my grandfather died at seventy-
seven, forty-five years after Ray Alexander shared*

Christ with him, I got burdened about it. So, at a family reunion, we went into a room alone, and I shared Christ with my grandfather, and my grandfather got saved. I called Ray Alexander. Ray didn't even know that my father got saved that night forty-five years before. I said to him, 'Because of you, thousands of people have come into the kingdom. And now I want you to know that my grandfather has been saved, too.' Ray Alexander started to weep. 'Your grandfather is the only name in the back of my Bible without a tick beside it.' He told me he had prayed for my grandfather for forty-five years, but as soon as he got off the phone, he was going to put a tick beside my grandfather's name.

Everyone on his list that he had been praying for had now come to Christ.

One of the mysteries regarding prayer is how some prayers are answered immediately, some take weeks or months, some years and years – while others remain (apparently) unanswered. I know what it is to put a brand-new prayer request to the Lord, write it down – expecting to repeat it daily indefinitely – only to have that request answered the same day! I can also tell you of many more requests that I have been bringing back to the Lord over and over again for the last twenty years – with no answer at all (that I can discern).

This is a mystery to me.

My dad used to tell me that his prayer for me as I was growing up was that I 'would not fall in love with the wrong girl'. This was a shrewd request. My father knew that once you fall in love, it is almost too late! Hence his wise prayer. That prayer was answered. Although I *thought* I was in love a couple of times – and got jilted a time or two – God spared me from falling truly in love until I met Louise. And, believe me, had she been the wrong girl, it was too late! Nobody could have stopped me!

And yet I know a lot of godly people who have prayed for their children – only to have them end up in disastrous marriages.

When my mother was taken seriously ill on 12 February 1953, my dad asked countless people to pray for her. She was anointed with oil at least five times. Several saintly people assured us that they had 'prayed through' regarding my mother, which is Kentucky jargon for God witnessing to them that my mother would be healed. One morning during his prayer time my dad felt that he received a strong witness from the Holy Spirit that my mother would live and not die. I myself got a verse of Scripture (which I took to be from the Lord) that convinced me that she would be healed. She died on 8 April 1953.

A few years later I came across a very important verse, one that has governed me no end: 'I will have mercy on whom I will have mercy, and I will have compassion on whom I will have compassion' (Exod. 33:19). This passage is foundational to understanding the sovereignty of God.

The sovereignty of God refers to God's prerogative to do what he pleases with whom he chooses. This covers every subject under the sun – salvation, healing, finances, relationships, gifts, callings, pay rises, jobs, guidance, and when he shows or hides his face. In a word: answered prayer begins with the sovereign will of God.

Yes, God may appear to change his mind, as in the illness and healing of Hezekiah (2 Kgs. 20:1–6); or in his declaration concerning destroying Nineveh (Jonah 3:9–10). And if I were Hezekiah or the king of Nineveh, I too would do what they did – plead with God with all my heart and soul! But I know at the same time that God will end up doing what he deems right in his own eyes, and we must trust his judgement, unwavering love and faithfulness when he does not come through for us in the way we wish he would. David knew in his heart that his child would die – as Nathan prophesied – but it did not stop David from begging God to spare the child (2 Sam. 12:14–23).

God answers prayer because he chooses to answer prayer, but it is *equally true* that God charges us with the responsibility to pray and plead with him as though the whole outcome were entirely up to us. Work that out! But that is the way it is. We are dealing with what Dr J. I. Packer calls an *antinomy* – two parallel principles that seem to be irreconcilable but are both true. In this case it means I will call on God over and over again regarding the same old requests – and yet know that underneath it all is his undeniable sovereignty. I can live with this; I hope you can too.

There are two principles that lie behind answered prayer: (1) any prayer that is prayed in the will of God will be answered, and (2) the shape that answered prayer takes is determined by our readiness at the time it is answered.

Principle One: any prayer prayed in the will of God will be answered

We have seen already that the only prayer that is 'heard' is that which is in accordance with God's will (1 John 5:15). What is meant by 'heard' by God is a request he takes on board; namely, when he chooses to honour our request. But we do not always know we are being heard, as we saw from our discussion on praying in the Spirit. It is therefore no disgrace not to know whether we are heard when we ask for particular things; Paul did not always know what to pray for, but trusted the intercession of the Spirit (Rom. 8:26–27).

Zechariah and Elizabeth prayed for a son. This was no doubt early in their marriage. They were heard, but they had no idea they had been heard. God did not notify them that they had been heard. They were not given the witness that what they prayed was exactly what God wanted. But years and years later they were unexpectedly given notice by the angel Gabriel that their prayers had been heard. 'Do not be afraid, Zechariah; your prayer has been heard' (Luke 1:13). I suspect Zechariah was thinking, 'Prayer? My prayer has been heard? What prayer?' The prayer that Gabriel referred to was probably prayed over twenty years before. Zechariah had no idea what Gabriel was talking about.

What Zechariah did not know was this. When he and Elizabeth asked for a son, God said 'yes'. That was in heaven, but they were on earth. They did not have a clue that God had said 'yes'; therefore after some twenty years had elapsed, it was a prayer request they had 'torn up', assuming it was time for them to move on with their lives.

Daniel had a similar experience, although the elapsed time was three weeks rather than twenty years. Daniel decided to fast and pray. He said that he 'mourned for three weeks. I ate no choice food; no meat or wine touched my lips; and I used no lotions at all until the three weeks were over' (Dan. 10:3). But an angel came to him and said in so many words, 'You were heard the very first day you prayed!' Indeed, 'Since the first day that you set your mind to gain understanding and to humble yourself before your God, *your words were heard*, and I have come in response to them' (emphasis mine, Dan. 10:12). If I were Daniel, I think I might have been tempted to say, cynically, 'Thanks a lot. Why have you made me wait for three weeks to know I had been heard? Why could you not have told me the first day as soon as I prayed?'

And why did God wait all those years before telling Zechariah his prayer had been heard? You tell me. It is a mystery.

We can only speculate as to why God answers prayer as he does, telling some people immediately that they have been heard, telling some later on that they have been heard, telling others nothing until God suddenly steps in and acts. God might have let Elizabeth get pregnant without the word from Gabriel. For some reason, God gave them advanced notice that this was going to happen.

So if we are going to speculate, why does God not always tell us whether we have been heard? I offer five reasons: (1) he likes our company, and not knowing exactly whether we have been heard keeps us coming back to him; (2) he lets us prove to ourselves how important our request is – so that we will keep asking if we really are serious about it; (3) that we do not waver in faith, and don't give up until it is absolutely clear that our request is not to be granted; (4) we will learn to think for ourselves, not unlike in Paul's admonition, 'Work out your salvation with fear and trembling, for it is God who works in you to will and to act according to his good purpose' (Phil. 2:12–13); (5) he wants to dignify us by our sharing in what he does through his kingdom on earth – namely, by our spreading the Word.

God likes our company. You will recall this thrilling truth that was put forward earlier in this book. God therefore has a way of drawing us back into his presence: to keep us asking. We probably wouldn't pray so hard if we did not need him to fulfil our desires. He likes our company so much that he withholds giving us what we want in order to get our attention. Can you cope with that? I can. Disappointed though I may be that God does not immediately grant what I want, the very thought that he is postponing my answered prayer because he likes my company warms my heart. I can live with this.

The problem was that Zechariah, although he observed all the Lord's commands and regulations blamelessly (Luke 1:6), was none the less quite wrong in his reaction to Gabriel's good news. He actually argued with Gabriel. Can you think of anything more stupid than arguing with Gabriel? I should think that if Gabriel came to me with a word, I would believe it! Or would I? All I know is that Zechariah had a quarrel going with Gabriel. 'How can I be sure of this? I am an old man and my wife is well on in years' (Luke 1:18).

How important is your prayer request? We need to say what we mean, and mean what we say when we talk to God. I know some people who ask God for something a couple of times – then forget about it. They find out later that God decided to grant their request – and they aren't ready for it. Perhaps they didn't really mean what they asked for. All I know is, we should be careful what we say in the presence of the Most High God. He listens. If we ask what is in his will, we are heard – right then, whether or not he tells us.

If we really mean what we say when we ask God for this or that, we will keep asking. It will not be a one-off request. We will prove how important our requests are by going back to God with them – as the widow did in Jesus' parable. She 'kept coming' with her plea, and she was commended for this (Luke 18:3–8).

We keep on believing. One of the most important principles in this connection are these words: 'Without faith it is impossible to please God, because anyone who comes to him must believe that he exists *and that he rewards those who earnestly seek him*' (emphasis mine, Heb. 11:6).

Zechariah was a good man, but he somehow lapsed into unbelief. The proof is that he was reprimanded for not believing what the angel Gabriel promised (Luke 1:20).

I am saying therefore that God withholds the knowledge of what he is going to do in order to test our faith. He wants us to be found believing him when he steps in to answer our request.

Learning to think clearly. Paul could not be present in Philippi all the time to answer any questions that might crop up, so he urged people to sort things out for themselves with fear and trembling. His command for them to work out their salvation was not regarding how to be saved but how salvation should be applied in their lives. There will always be questions, and we may not have authority figures around to give us answers. So Paul told them to work through things for themselves when he was not there;

after all, 'it is God who works in you to will and to act according to his good purpose' (Phil. 2:12–13).

When we are waiting for God to act it is the same as being 'between the times'. It is then that we can learn a lot. God gave us brains and he wants us to use them. We all must learn to think – and to think clearly. It pleases and honours him when we, in fear and trembling, come up with our best judgement when we have nobody we can turn to – or if God himself is hiding his face from us.

In other words, God withholds clear communication from us sometimes in order that we will please him by sound thinking. This is how we develop leadership skills as well.

God wants to dignify us by our role in his kingdom. God has invited us to spread his kingdom around the world – both in numbers and in qualitative growth. In God's wisdom he was pleased to save his people by the foolishness of what is preached (1 Cor. 1:21), and yet they are not saved apart from our spreading the Word. 'How, then, can they call on the one they have not believed in? And how can they believe in the one of whom they have not heard? And how can they hear without someone preaching to them?' (Rom. 10:14). We are commanded to preach the gospel to every person and make disciples out of them (Matt. 28:19).

Prayer is a vital part of spreading the gospel. 'Pray also for me,' said Paul, 'that whenever I open my mouth, words may be given me so that I will fearlessly make known the mystery of the gospel' (Eph. 6:19).

There is therefore a kind of praying that requires consistent, persistent and constant intercession. God does not let us off the hook by saying, 'Enough – stop praying.' No.

I therefore submit all the above propositions as possible reasons why God does not always assure us in advance of all he is going to do. I conclude, then, that there are good reasons that God does not tell us when we have prayed in his will. I only know this for sure: any prayer that is prayed in the will of God will be answered – sooner or later.

Principle Two: the shape that answered prayer takes is determined by our readiness

But there is a second major principle: the shape that answered prayer takes is determined by our *readiness at the time* God actually steps in to act. Nothing will stop God from answering the prayer that was prayed in his will; any prayer prayed within the will of God will be answered. You can count on that. But the shape it takes is determined by whether we are in faith or unbelief at the time that God answers.

Zechariah wasn't ready. What ought to have been his finest hour turns out to be his most embarrassing moment. The angel Gabriel says to Zechariah, 'Your prayer has been heard. Your wife Elizabeth will bear you a son . . . And now you will be silent and not able to speak until the day this happens, *because you did not believe my words*, which will come true at their proper time' (emphasis mine, Luke 1:13, 20).

Even Zechariah's unbelief did not stop answered prayer. But his unbelief determined the shape that answered prayer took: he was struck dumb and not able to speak.

You can imagine his embarrassment when friends came to congratulate him when the word was out that Elizabeth was pregnant. He could not enjoy this – he was humiliated with this strange impediment; he couldn't talk!

But his prayer was answered, and John the Baptist was born. But the shape the whole scenario took was shaped by Zechariah's folly, and he was not allowed to enjoy it.

You could not have told Zechariah years before that he was going to have a son but that he would be less than happy about it all. He would have said, 'If I knew that I was going to be the father of a son, I would be a very happy and fulfilled man. Nothing could make me unhappy if I knew I would have a son.' And yet the news of the very thing he wanted so much was met with sadness.

The shape that answered prayer takes is determined by our readiness at the time.

At the end of his parable about the widow's persistence, Jesus posed a question: 'when the Son of Man comes, will he find faith on the earth?' (Luke 18:8) This striking question is put at the end of this parable not only with reference to the Second Coming, but also because one could start out praying in faith and end up in unbelief. After giving the parable about the persistent woman, Jesus applied it: 'Will not God bring about justice for his chosen ones, who cry out to him day and night? Will he keep putting them off? I tell you, he will see that they get justice, and quickly. However, when the Son of Man comes, will he find faith on the earth?' (Luke 18:7–8) In other words, what would it have been like had the widow given up? But she didn't give up, and neither must we. If God answers our prayer but finds us in unbelief, it will diminish the joy that should be ours.

I can remember a man called Marvin who started a church in Ashland, Kentucky. He, along with his wife and another couple, rented a garage in which they held services. They prayed that they might have their own building. People laughed at them, and many felt the church should not have been started. But several years later their prayer was answered. Their numbers grew and they erected one of the finest buildings in the southern part of Ashland. They brought in the general superintendent of their denomination for the day of the dedication. The place was packed with some four hundred people. In the meantime, Marvin had fallen out with the rest of the church, and on the day of the dedication Marvin was not even welcome in this church. They said he drove past the church and saw the people coming in – but he kept on driving. His prayer was answered, but there was a cloud over the day – at least for him.

The prayer of Isaiah, 'Oh, that you would rend the heavens and come down' (Isa. 64:1) was the heart-cry in every synagogue in ancient Israel for hundreds of years as they prayed for their Messiah to come. He came, but they did not recognise him. Jesus wept over the city of Jerusalem which had rejected him and lamented, 'If you, even you, had only known on this day what would bring you peace – but now it is hidden from your eyes . . . you did not recognise the time of God's coming to you' (Luke 19:42, 44).

Israel's prayer was answered, but it was shaped by their readiness at the time. They *weren't* ready – that is why they missed their Messiah.

We must say what we mean and mean what we say when we pray – and stay at it. Do not ever forget that Jesus gave that parable to show that we should 'always pray and not give up' (Luke 18:1).

Ask yourself: what is it you once asked for – but stopped asking for? Praying for a loved one? A different job? A husband or wife? To have children? Healing? Revival? A new home? You may say: 'There is no way God could answer any of these requests and it will be under a cloud if it is answered.' I reply: don't be so sure; the shape that answered prayer takes is determined by our readiness at the time. God wants you to be found believing when he steps in.

A Scottish couple came up to me at the Garden Tomb in Jerusalem right after my sermon there. 'Do you recognise us?' they asked. 'No, sorry!' I smiled. 'Well, you preached a sermon in Edinburgh called "Are you Ready for Answered Prayer?" about Zechariah and Elizabeth.' 'Yes, of course,' I said. 'Well, that sermon convicted us. We had given up hope that we would ever get to come to Israel. That night we began praying once more that we might get to come to the Holy Land – and here we are! And fancy meeting you here!' What a lovely thing the Lord did for them – and me!

Perhaps God will use this chapter to motivate you to go back to that old prayer list – and recommence praying through it! Until God gives a definite, absolute and irrevocable 'No', keep praying and assume the answer may be 'Yes'.

Why, then, does God ask us to pray when he already knows what we need – and has promised to look after us? Why pray?

The best answer to the question 'Why pray?' is this: God asks us to – and commands it. This is good enough for me.

We referred to the antinomy earlier – parallel principles that seem irreconcilable but both are true. The question regarding the sovereignty of God and evangelism is that if God knows in advance who will be saved, why should we try to convert everybody? The answer is: because we are commanded to (Matt. 28:19; 2 Cor. 5:19–20). That too is good enough for me.

Isaac had God's oath that his seed would be as the sand of the sea, but his wife Rebekah was barren. What did Isaac do? 'Isaac prayed to the LORD on behalf of his wife, because she was barren' (Gen. 25:21).

Therefore if God asks me to pray, even though he knows the future perfectly and my need backwards and forwards, I will pray. Yes, 'your Father knows what you need before you ask him' (Matt. 6:8), but *I will tell him anyway*. In the exact same way that the Lord may know we are grateful, but wants us to *tell him*, so too I will pour out my heart to him as if I were informing him.

Jesus said we must come to the Father as a child would (Matt. 18:3). A child does not have sophisticated theological knowledge. A child does not say, 'If God knows the future, why pray?' Small children don't ask, 'Why does God allow suffering?' or 'What's the point of telling God what he already knows?' A child does not know that prayer is a mystery; he or she simply comes to Jesus and trusts him. So must we. Can you do that? If you want to be proficient in prayer, be like a child.

Here is a wonderful verse: 'Trust in the LORD with all your heart and *lean not on your own understanding*' (emphasis mine, Prov. 3:5). You will never know how many times that verse has bailed me out of difficulty. My understanding of a situation has been enough to keep me from praying a thousand times! But I would instead meditate on Proverbs 3:5 – and keep praying and trusting the Lord. One of the darkest hours Louise and I ever went through was on the night of 16 January 1985. It was the most historic church meeting in Westminster Chapel's history and the hall was packed. People came to vote who hadn't ever come to hear me preach, but they were there to take sides with a group of people who were determined to end my pastorate. It was over (so I thought). I heard an inner voice – not quite audible, but almost: 'do not lean on your own understanding'. But moments later the vote that was to end my ministry turned out to silence my opposition. We stayed there another seventeen years.

If you want to be a good prayer warrior, don't try to work things out! Don't let sophisticated issues enter into your thinking. When Rodney Howard-Browne came to Westminster Chapel saying that some of us needed a 'head bypass operation', many were horrified, but I knew exactly what he meant – and he was right.

Why pray? Martin Luther said, 'We are instructing ourselves, not God.' John Calvin said, 'We do not pray with the view of informing God but in order that we may arouse ourselves to seek him.' John Wesley said, 'God does nothing but in answer to prayer.'

If John Wesley is right, then things will not happen until we seek God's face – and ask him to act.

By the way, don't worry about asking God for small things; with God, everything is small.

Why pray? It is sheer obedience to God's Word.

Why pray? God who ordained the end equally ordained the means to the end. The same God who said, 'I make known the end from the beginning, from ancient times, what is still to come' (Isa. 46:10), also said, 'Call to me and I will answer you and tell you great and unsearchable things you do not know' (Jer. 33:3).

Yes, prayer is an unfathomable mystery, but only a fool would refuse to pray because he or she cannot figure things out in advance.

Prayer is for *us*, not God; it keeps us humble. In fact, perhaps the greatest thing that can be said about prayer is that it keeps us humble. It puts us on our knees, remembering who God is. 'God is in heaven and you are on earth' (Eccles. 5:2).

Why pray? God chose to honour our obedience. Logic says, since he knows our need and promised to supply it, there is no need to pray. God doesn't honour our logic; he honours our obedience. The truth is, 'You do not have, because you do not ask' (James 4:2). As Charles H. Spurgeon used to say, 'When I don't pray, coincidences don't happen; when I pray, coincidences happen.'

Why pray? God knows our need but dignifies us by letting our praying make a difference. *Prayer changes things*. God gives us the privilege of changing things. We can have a hand in diverting a disaster. We can have a hand in moving God's heart. As Jacob said, when he realised he was wrestling with God, 'I will not let you go unless you bless me' (Gen. 32:26).

Why pray? Because God promises to answer prayer. His honour is at stake; his integrity is at stake; his Word is at stake.

It is we who need this thing called prayer, not God.

15

Unanswered Prayer

Three times I pleaded with the Lord to take it
away from me. (2 Cor. 12:8)

In this concluding chapter I raise the question, and will
attempt to answer it in part, of why the God of the Bible,
being a God of purest integrity who cannot lie (Heb. 6:18;
Titus 1:2), often appears not to answer our prayers even
though he has promised to do so.

Before his death, resurrection and ascension to heaven,
Jesus gave some wonderful promises: 'I will do whatever you
ask in my name, so that the Son may bring glory to the
Father. You may ask me for anything in my name, and I will
do it' (John 14:13–14). 'If you remain in me and my words
remain in you, ask whatever you wish, and it will be given
you' (John 15:7). In addition to these, Paul said: 'He who did
not spare his own Son, but gave him up for us all – how will

he not also, along with him, graciously give us all things' (Rom. 8:32). John added, 'Dear friends, if our hearts do not condemn us, we have confidence before God and receive from him anything we ask, because we obey his commands and do what pleases him' (1 John 3:21–22). A thousand years before, David said, 'Delight yourself in the LORD and he will give you the desires of your heart' (Ps. 37:4).

I know of a man by the name of Kelly who was on death row in a prison in South Carolina. He was converted a few months before his scheduled execution. He began to read his Bible and came across the words, 'If ye ask anything in my name, I will do it' (John 14:14 – AV). He began to pray that he would not have to die in the electric chair, for he knew he was innocent of the crime of which he had been convicted. He showed the verse to the Nazarene pastor who had led him to Christ. The pastor began to explain to this new Christian that he should go a bit slow in trying to claim this promise for such a great wish – receiving a pardon from the governor of the state of South Carolina. But, said the prisoner, 'Jesus clearly tells me in John 14:14 that if I ask anything in his name, I will receive.' The pastor nervously tried to encourage the new convert who stuck to his guns – 'I will not have to die, this word says so.' The pastor was very worried that the new Christian would lose his faith. Whenever the pastor went to the prisoner's cell for a visit, he would always find the prisoner kneeling on his Bible with it opened to John 14:14. Minutes before the scheduled execution, as the handcuffed prisoner was being escorted to the electric chair, the governor pardoned the prisoner. Kelly became an evangelist and told his story all over America.

Not all have this kind of experience with John 14:14, however. And, if it worked every time in the way that it did for Kelly, probably the whole world would be Christians. There would be no offence to the Christian faith; everyone would gladly relinquish their previous biases if they could get a free ticket to the things they want in life by calling on God in Jesus' name.

When Paul knew he was going to Corinth he made a calculated decision: not to emphasise the power of prayer, or other fringe benefits from being a Christian, or a promise like John 14:14, but instead 'to know nothing while I was with you except Jesus Christ and him crucified' (1 Cor. 2:2). It no doubt limited Paul's reception there, but Paul only wanted the gospel to be believed – not other things that are included in the Christian package.

Prayer is the new Christian's discovery, but it is not always the best way to introduce people to Jesus. Why is this? All who transfer their trust in good works to the shed blood of Christ are saved; but not all who are saved get what they want when they pray. I can appreciate the South Carolina pastor's concern that his new convert might become discouraged.

Theologian Paul Tillich used to talk about the 'ontological shock' – *why is there something and not nothing?* I don't think everybody thinks that deeply, but I do know that every new Christian under the sun sooner or later experiences for himself or herself a feeling of being betrayed by God. It can come in any number of ways, but one of them is when you pray and things don't happen when you thought they would.

I only know that not all prayers are answered as people initially wish, and no doubt the released prisoner I referred to above, once he was out of prison and had begun preaching, discovered that John 14:14 did not work every time as it had done just before his scheduled execution.

I am so glad that Paul shared with us that he had a thorn in the flesh and that he prayed three times for it to go away – and it never did. If you are interested in the various ways a thorn in the flesh can be ours too, please see my book *Thorn in the Flesh*.

I will now come to the heart of my thesis in this chapter: that unanswered prayer is God's deliberate *answer* to prayer as much as any answered prayer is. Deliberate? Yes. He gives as much attention to his denial of our request as he does approval of it.

Unanswered prayer is therefore part of God's answer to our prayer. Although it was not the response Paul was hoping for, God answered Paul's request that the thorn in the flesh be removed: 'My grace is sufficient for you, for my power is made perfect in weakness' (2 Cor. 12:9). Nothing passes by the throne of grace without God's careful attention. He acts upon every request that comes to him in the name of his Son.

You don't have to be the Apostle Paul to get God's attention. God loves every person as if there were no one else to love and answers every prayer that comes to him in Jesus' name. It is only that you may not like his answer – at first.

But why did Jesus promise that God would grant our own particular requests that are put to him in Jesus' name – but apparently doesn't? I will try to answer this. There are a lot of things I don't know, but I will share some things that I *do* know.

I know that I have lived long enough to thank God for unanswered prayer. In fact, the longer I live, the more I thank him for the prayers he did not answer with 'yes'. As Alec Motyer put it, if God was compelled to answer all my prayers with 'yes', I would never have the courage to pray for anything else again. It took me a while, however, to come to this place.

Several years ago there was a popular country and western song called 'Thank God for unanswered prayer'. It was written by a man who had been jilted by his childhood sweetheart – but prayed to get her back – and ran into her several years later. When he saw what she now looked like and what she had turned out to be, he wrote the song, 'Thank God for unanswered prayer'. As I mentioned earlier, I too know what it feels like to be jilted – more than once in my youth – and prayed at that time to win these girlfriends back. I am *so* glad God did not answer my prayer, but gave me Louise later on.

I conclude therefore that what prayers I am *still* putting

to God all the time – yes, daily – will be answered if such is best for me. And what is not best for me will not be answered – that is, answered my way.

I base my premise on personal testimony and Scripture.

Let me begin with Scripture. Jesus had a close friend – named Lazarus. Lazarus' two sisters Mary and Martha sent word to Jesus that their brother was extremely ill. When they sent that word to Jesus they believed that he would stop what he was doing (whatever it was and wherever he was) and make his way to Bethany and heal Lazarus. They took this for granted.

Jesus received the word in plenty of time to make it to Bethany to keep Lazarus from dying. Jesus could even have healed Lazarus from a distance by 'remote control' – as he had done before. But Jesus made no attempt to go to Bethany, nor did he pray for Lazarus to be healed. He stayed put. His response was that Lazarus' sickness would not end in death but was for the glory of God and his Son (John 11:4).

Jesus gave a further reason to his disciples regarding why he stayed behind and did not go to Bethany: 'so that you may believe'. They could not understand what was happening – that Jesus was refusing to heal Lazarus. But Jesus said to them plainly, 'Lazarus is dead, and for your sake I am glad I was not there,' adding, '*so that you may believe*' (emphasis mine, John 11:14–15).

You may recall that I touched on this in Chapter 6. I now return to emphasise it because it is essential for a right understanding of unanswered prayer. Not only that; it is one of the most important verses in the Bible regarding the nature of true faith. Faith to be *faith* is believing God without empirical evidence. 'Faith is being sure of what we hope for and certain of what we do not see' (Heb. 11:1). If you have the evidence and then you say, 'Now I believe,' such 'belief' does not warrant the title 'faith'. It is only faith when you have no objective explanation for believing, but believe none the less.

Therefore when Jesus said, 'I am glad I was not there, so that you may believe,' he meant that he was doing them a most wonderful favour; he was going to teach them a lesson in faith. Had Jesus taken off for Bethany and healed Lazarus, this would not have come as a surprise, or even if he healed Lazarus by 'remote control'. But what surprised them was that he did nothing.

When God does *nothing* and we still trust him, that is *faith*.

Jesus showed up in Bethany four days after the funeral. Both Mary and Martha were bewildered and said: 'Lord, if you had been here, my brother would not have died' (John 11:21, 32).

This was a case of unanswered prayer. They sent for Jesus; that is prayer. Jesus did not come; that is unanswered prayer.

But Jesus had a better idea and yet kept it to himself at first: let's raise Lazarus from the dead, which is what he did (John 11:43–44). What Jesus ended up doing was far grander and more glorious than merely keeping Lazarus from dying. In other words, had Jesus answered their prayer they would never have known what he might have done, for their answered prayer would have been far, far short of what God had in mind.

We therefore should never underestimate what God could be up to when we don't get our way immediately. Unanswered prayer could be a hint that God is thinking of something that will bring him greater glory than if he answered our prayer. That is what was partly at stake when Jesus did not heal Lazarus, but raised him from the dead instead. God postponed Israel's deliverance from Pharaoh with a reason: 'I will harden the hearts of the Egyptians so that they will go in after them. And I will gain glory through Pharaoh and all his army' (Exod. 14:17).

When you are perplexed that God seems to turn a deaf ear to your plea, consider this: he is coming up with ways to gain glory for himself. The more glory he gets, the better off you and I are! Mary and Martha had no complaints when they saw what Jesus had in mind from the start. Moses could only rejoice in the way all things turned out in ancient Egypt.

So will you.

The unanswered prayer of Mary and Martha was as much an answer from God as what they initially prayed for. Jesus' delay was based on a plan that had been thought through. Therefore the decision to stay away from Bethany for a few days and let Lazarus die was deliberate.

Whenever God says 'no' it may be because he has a better idea than the one we had requested. What God actually has in mind is worth waiting for. You can go to the bank with this.

Therefore when you read verses like John 14:14 and God does not come through for you, you are understandably perplexed. But God is glad for your sake; the disappointment gives you a chance to believe. The non-believer says 'seeing is believing', but the Bible says that if you can see, you have ruled out faith as a possibility. God does us an incalculable favour when he withholds what we want from him; it is our moment to trust him. Job could not understand all that was going on in his life, but he came through with flying colours: 'Though he slay me, yet will I hope in him' (Job 13:15). God wants that for you and me.

I reckon I have seen more accomplished in my own life through my unanswered prayers than I have my answered prayers. Or to put it another way: as I look back on my life over the past fifty years, I strongly suspect that unanswered prayer has been the chief way that God has answered my most important prayers. Not *all* of my prayers – my most important ones. After all, some requests are more important than others.

Here is the way it works. God uses our natural wants to get our attention. We put our requests to him – some are exactly in his will, others are not. I can look back over my life and recall certain things I asked for when I was younger: to get the girlfriend I wanted (almost always at the top of the list!), to become a trial lawyer (a desire I had as a teenager), to catch a fish (when I went fishing), for Joe DiMaggio (my baseball hero) to hit a home run (when I watched the New York Yankees on TV), to meet Joe DiMaggio, for the New York Yankees to win, to meet Arthur Rubenstein (the pianist – another hero), to get all A's on my report card, to get a superior rating when I played an oboe solo, to meet Billy Graham (yet another hero), for God to heal my mother, for people to come to the altar and be saved when the pastor or evangelist preached, to know whether I was called to preach or not (after I left home and went to Trevecca Nazarene University), to get one particular girlfriend (a different one) to marry me, to help me preach a good sermon (now I knew I had been called to preach).

My point is this. All these requests (regardless of how they sound to someone else!) were extremely important to me at the time. God knew this. I would plead John 14:14 as the reason God should answer me. Some of the above requests were granted, others were not. I survived. God got my attention through these, enticing me to spend time with him. The more I spent time with him, the more I learned to say 'Yes, Lord' when I did not get what I wanted at the time. But I got to know the Lord more and more.

But what about John 14:14 – is it true or not? 'You may ask me for *anything* in my name, *and I will do it*' (emphasis mine). I did not become a trial lawyer, and the girlfriend I prayed to marry didn't become my wife, I never met Arthur

Rubenstein, and my mother was not healed. So did God lie to me in John 14:14?

The phrase people overlook are these words: 'in my name'. The name of God is not to be used as a magic wand that you wave over a request. Some think that the mere mention of 'Jesus' ensures you can ask for anything from a Rolls-Royce, to healing, to win the election, to have tea with the Queen or win the Lottery – since God must honour Jesus' name.

What we forget is that God's name is 'Jealous': 'Do not worship any other god, for the LORD, whose name is Jealous, is a jealous God' (Exod. 34:14).

Truly to pray in Jesus' name is to *submit* to the name of God. It is not a name to be used for our manipulative, selfish purposes as if it were a good luck charm. To pray in the name of Jesus is to embrace him as he is – and submit to all he wants.

James said, 'When you ask, you do not receive, because you ask with wrong motives, that you may spend what you get on your pleasures' (James 4:3). What many have done in this 'me generation' is to lift passages from God's infallible Word and apply them to situations absolutely alien to the purpose of those passages.

Take for example these words of Jesus: 'Ask and it will be given to you; seek and you will find; knock and the door will be opened to you. For everyone who asks receives; he who seeks finds; and to him who knocks, the door will be opened' (Matt. 7:7–8). These words are from Jesus' sermon on the mount, and the context is the kingdom of heaven. This is to be desired above all else. When Jesus said these words, 'Ask and it will be given to you,' he assumed that those who listened (or read) what came before, actually *wanted* the kingdom to come. The trouble is that people sometimes come from a worldly perspective, then seize certain words and apply them to a situation that is devoid of wanting to honour God's Word.

That is not all; compare Matthew 7:7–11 with Luke 11:9–13. These parallel passages are virtually verbatim. In Matthew's account, Jesus' words are, 'If you then, though you are evil, know how to give good gifts to your children, how much more will your Father in heaven give *good gifts* to those who ask him!' (emphasis mine, Matt. 7:11) The words 'good gifts' are replaced by 'the Holy Spirit' in Luke 11:13: 'If you then, though you are evil, know how to give good gifts to your children, how much more will your Father in heaven give *the Holy Spirit* to those who ask him!' (emphasis mine) Those who read Matthew's account might lift out the words 'good gifts' to mean *whatever we want*, but Luke's words 'the Holy Spirit' clearly show that Jesus had not carnal matters in mind, but spiritual things.

Furthermore, John 14:14 equally refers to the Holy Spirit. These words are right in the middle of Jesus' effort to help the disciples make the transition from the level of nature (having him with them) to the level of the Spirit (John 14:9–16:33). He is about to tell them he is going away and that the Comforter, our Advocate, the Holy Spirit, will come alongside. By inviting us to ask 'anything in my name' in John 14:14, Jesus primarily means praying for anything spiritual. In John 14:12 Jesus said, 'I tell you the truth, anyone who has faith in me will do what I have been doing. He will do even greater things than these, because I am going to the Father.' I must admit I have a lot to learn regarding this verse, but it is surely referring to our following in Jesus' steps after his ascension into heaven. It is not a blank cheque that we ask God to sign and we fill in all our natural desires. This would indeed mean 'asking amiss, that ye may consume it upon your lusts' (James 4:3 – AV).

At the right hand of God is our Great High Priest, Jesus the Son of God (Heb. 4:14). He is seated there and makes intercession on our behalf. He is there, ever beckoning the attention of the Father to himself to keep his gaze 'away from our sins', as Calvin put it. Jesus filters our requests that come to him. He does not pass on our requests to the Father that are not in the Father's will. Jesus *knows* the Father's will. He knows what to put through to the Father and what to dismiss. Since we can only get to the Father through Jesus, all our requests go through him. He protects us from ourselves. He makes sure that our ill-posed requests don't reach the Father's heart – lest we are brought to leanness of soul (Ps. 106:15 – AV). In other words, Jesus at God's right hand is doing us a great favour by keeping our bad or foolish requests from being passed on. Jesus only intercedes according to the will of God.

And yet we are indeed allowed to ask for anything on our hearts – even those things that are not spiritual. The proof of this is in Jesus' parable of the persistent widow in Luke 18:1–8. Her request was not spiritual: 'Grant me justice against my adversary' (v. 3). That example encourages me no end to ask God for literally *anything* that may be on my heart. I will no doubt ask for many things out of his will, but not to worry. That is one of the big things that our Great High Priest does for us; he filters our prayers *so that the ill-posed requests are never heard.*

Therefore when I claim John 14:14 when I pray – and I always do – I at the same time submit to him whose name is Jealous. He only wants what is right in his eyes, and that is all I want in any case. The point is, I don't use John 14:14 to get God to do what he doesn't want to do; I want him to do what he wants to do.

In the same section in which James talks about asking with wrong motives he also mentions the Spirit working in us jealously (James 4:5). We have a jealous God who loves us infinitely more than we love ourselves, overruling us as needs be to keep us from getting our way when it wouldn't be good for us.

All that I am saying in this chapter coheres with two of the greatest promises of all regarding prayer. First, Psalm 37:4: 'Delight yourself in the LORD and he will give you the desires of your heart.' Many of us take the second part of that verse and run with it! Wow – I can have the desires of my heart! Yes, but this assumes that, first of all, we have delighted ourselves in the Lord. As St Augustine put it long ago, 'Love God and do what you please.' But if you truly love God, what you are pleased to do will honour him, not dishonour him. So too with prayer. When we delight ourselves in the *Lord*, we will want what he wants.

The second passage is 1 John 3:21–22: 'Dear friends, if our hearts do not condemn us, we have confidence before God and receive from him anything we ask, because we obey his commands and do what pleases him.' In other words, when we obey his commands and do what pleases him, anything we ask will be in accordance with his will – not against his will.

And yet when we get it wrong – and we will – we have an Advocate at God's right hand who will make sure our bad requests are not heard.

This is why unanswered prayer is answered prayer. We simply get a different answer from the one we wanted at first.

I am so thankful that God has saved me from myself thousands of times over the years. I am so grateful for unanswered prayer or, rather, *his* answer to my fleshly wish.

For example, instead of removing a bad situation in Westminster Chapel (my solution), the Lord taught me to 'dignify the trial' (James 1:2). That has turned out to be one of the best things that ever happened to me and, also, one of the sweetest insights I have ever had. As Charles Colson put it, God does not promise to take us out of the fire; he promises to get into the fire with us. Moreover, instead of sending revival to Westminster Chapel – which I wanted more than anything – he taught me that I needed to be more like Jesus (Phil. 2:5). I blush to admit that I preferred revival – at first. Instead of vindicating me over my enemies (oh yes, Lord, please!), he taught me total forgiveness (Matt. 5:44). I now prefer *his* answer to my prayer over anything you could name. Instead of granting a hundred things I had requested – which I thought would make me happier – he opened my mind so that I could understand the Scriptures (Luke 24:45). Instead of giving us the kind of retirement we dreamed of, he opened doors all over the world I had never dreamed of (1 Cor. 16:9). Instead of giving me the prestigious invitations I used to want in the flesh, he gave me breakthroughs in the Spirit that were far, far more satisfying (John 16:13). Instead of letting me develop friendships with respected people that I thought would make me look good – which I tried to make happen – he let me make surprising friendships without my making it happen (Matt. 23:12).

You may have thought that the possibility of unanswered prayer is the greatest reason not to pray. Wrong. I believe that quite the opposite is the case.

In the aforementioned Prayer Covenant I introduced at Westminster Chapel, we had five petitions. The fifth was: that each of us who agreed to the covenant would become more like Jesus. It was Arthur Blessitt who persuaded me to add that one. Wow. I am ashamed to admit that I had not even thought of that petition, but I am so thankful for it. I cannot say I am like Jesus, but I can say I am more like him than I was. As John Newton once said to William Cowper, 'I am not what I ought to be. I am not what I want to be. I am not what I hope to be. But thank God I am not what I used to be.' Becoming more like Jesus suits God more than a thousand requests I could come up with. The amazing irony is, the more I aspire to be like Jesus, the more I receive things that I had not even counted on. I will say it again: God only wants what is best for us. My dad's favourite verse in the Bible was: 'But seek ye first the kingdom of God, and his righteousness; and all these things shall be added unto you' (Matt. 6:33 – AV).

Prayer, the greatest fringe benefit of being a Christian, is God's enticement to get our attention. He likes our company.

What is more, sometimes we do have our cake and eat it too. He gives us some of the very things we wanted – in his way. I did not get the girlfriends I wanted when I was young. But he gave me Louise – the best of the lot. He did not heal my mother, but that event shaped my life and ministry and proved whether I would still serve God if she died. I did not become a lawyer but a preacher instead – and I am happy with this. He even let the New York Yankees win quite often, and one day I met Joe DiMaggio too! And I had the privilege of getting to know Billy Graham.

Seek his kingdom first, then you can be sure God will

look after all your needs – plus throwing in other nice things along the way.

Unanswered prayer is the best thing that could happen to us, because this way we get what God says we need. It is always better than what we thought we wanted.

And most of all, we get to know him. How kind he is to stoop to our weakness, all because he likes our company. How wonderful he is. 'Many, O LORD my God, are the wonders you have done. The things you planned for us no one can recount to you; were I to speak and tell of them, they would be too many to declare' (Ps. 40:5). There is nothing more amazing than God's love and care for each of us. But we learn to enjoy and appreciate his love in proportion to how much we pray and spend time with him.

So the worst thing of all is not to pray at all. Forgetting to enquire of the Lord will result in endless confusion and disappointment.

Before you left your room this morning, did you think to pray?

May the blessing of God Almighty – Father, Son and Holy Spirit – be yours, now and always. Amen.